# Carole Tolila

## with Camille Gressier

# FLOWERS

***This is a book to leaf through …***

In your hands is a 'book-as-object'. In *FLOWERS*, you can learn more about 30 flowers for which I happen to have a soft spot, while at the same time discovering the graphic worlds of 30 international artists. But every one of these illustrations is so beautiful that it would be a shame to just hide it away in a book, never to see the light of day. For this reason, I wanted to create a book from which you could, without a single pang of guilt, remove any pages you like and hang them on your wall. With a little strip of decorative tape or a charming picture frame, you will be able to bring the beauty of nature and a little bit of poetry into your home.

This book is special not only because of its form but because of its contents: it is a collective work. Within its pages you will find 30 visions of nature by 30 women illustrators, some well known, others perhaps less so – at the budding stages of their careers. They come, too, from every corner of the globe, and every kind of creativity is present in these pages, each illustration paying homage to the unsurpassed genius of nature.

Before I let you wander through my field of flowers, allow me to introduce myself. I am a journalist and the host of *Silence, ça pousse!*, a beloved gardening programme in France, as well as *Pyjama Thérapie*, a cosy home decor Instagram series. Camille Gressier ably aided me in the art direction of this book, and our shared hope is to make your walls bloom, so please don't hesitate to share photos of your handiwork with us: @carole_tolila @camille_gressier #flowersthebook.

**ilex**

IN ORDER OF APPEARANCE, THE FLOWER ILLUSTRATIONS ARE THE WORK OF:

PEONY, @lemonscarletgalerie

DELPHINIUM, @manoncardin_illustrations

NIGELLA, @briandafjstuart

AGAPANTHUS, @anna_illustrations

DAHLIA, @flora.roberts

CAMELLIA, @cath_stonehouse

LILY OF THE VALLEY, @adelinechemin

WILD CHICORY, @florawaycott

SNOWDROP, @makitoy

TULIP, @lapoireimaginaire

PASSION FLOWER, @becomingamorningperson

ROSE, @emilyisabella

HEATHER, @isabellelaydierkristensen

POINSETTIA, @beckyamelia_art

ROCKROSE, @juliebor91

ANEMONE, @alexandra.bodji

IRIS, @m_a_n_d_y_s_a_d_e

SEA HOLLY, @lucypanes

POPPY, @liliarnorldstudios

GRAPE HYACINTH, @sarahgordondesign

SCABIOUS, @mimizchao

CROCUS, @caitlinmcgauley

MIMOSA, @agathem.illustration

FREESIA, @whiteheartdesign

RUSSIAN SAGE, @kaysillustrations

FRITILLARY, @rosieharbottle

PANSY, @helendealtry

LILAC, @shealeenlouise

HELLEBORE, @claudialowry_art

COSMOS, @gracegillespieart

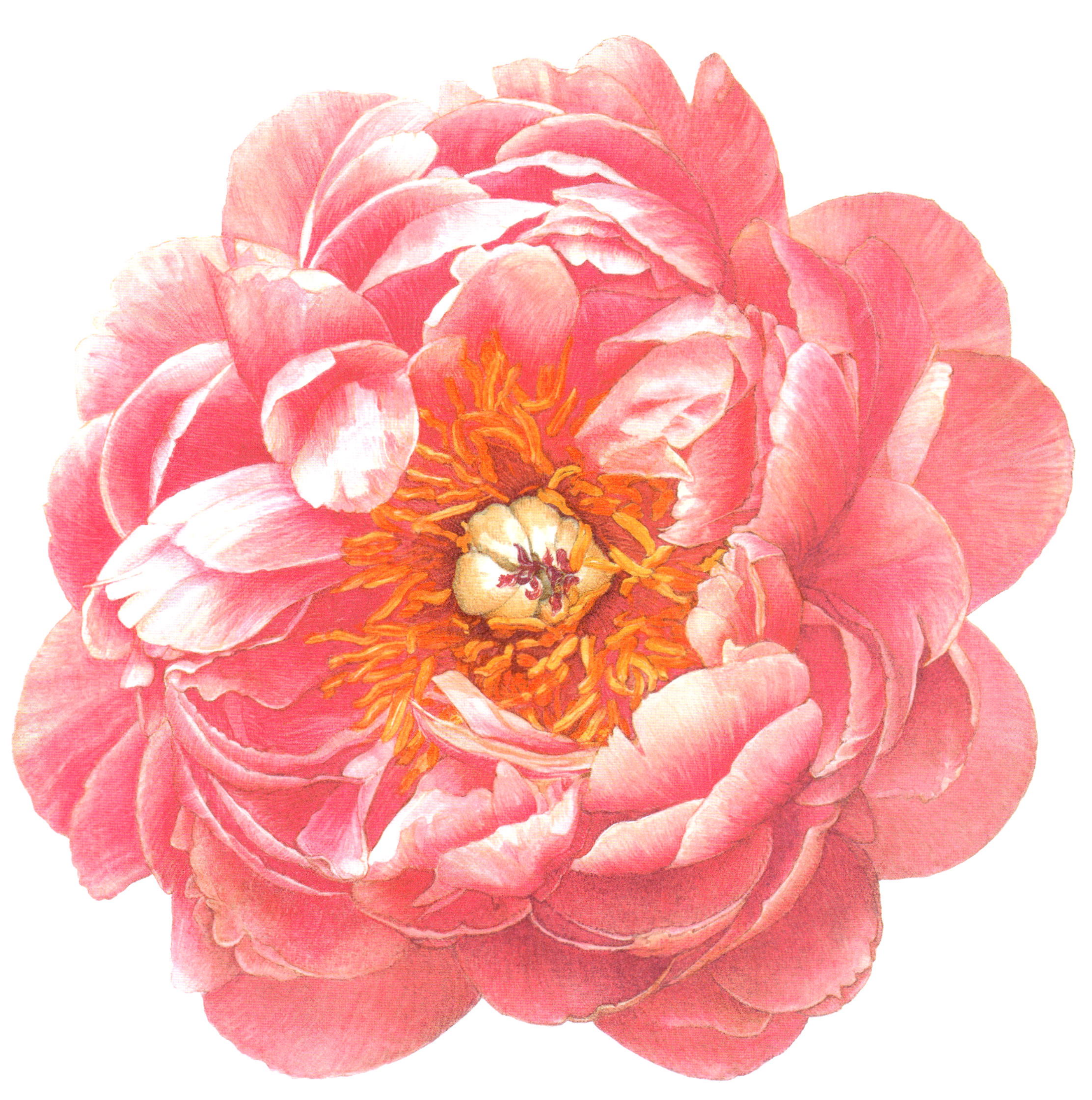

HERBACIOUS PEONY OR
THE KING OF FLOWERS

---

**BOTANICAL
FAMILY:**
PAEONIACEAE.

---

**BLOOMS:**
MID-APRIL
FOR EARLY VARIETIES;
END OF MAY FOR THE
LATER ONES.

---

**WHEN TO PLANT:**
OCTOBER TO APRIL.

---

**COLOURS:**
PINK, RED, PEACH,
WHITE, BICOLOURED.

**V**oluptuous, sensual, dazzling … there is no shortage of adjectives to describe the peony. It may bloom only briefly, but it knows how to get our attention when it does. To bring peonies into one's life is to recall the brevity of one's earthly existence. Yet, in Japan the 'king of flowers' symbolizes honour and good fortune.

There are a very large number of herbaceous peonies, which, unlike the tree peonies, have supple, rather than woody, stems. My favourite peonies are:

• 'Coral Sunset' whose colour varies, most notably with age
• The astonishing 'Gay Paree' with its double ring of large rose-pink guard petals surrounding a central creamy pompom
• The *lactiflora* 'Chiffon Parfait' with its bewitching beauty and a lifespan of up to 50 years.

You might also consider the 'Sarah Bernhardt', perhaps the best-known variety, or 'Dreamtime', which, in 2024, won the American Peony Society's 'Flower of the Year'.

When planting, remember that the peony generally needs a little time to bed in and perhaps won't flower straight away. The herbaceous peony prefers sunny spots, although some varieties will tolerate semi-shade. It needs well-aerated, cool, rich soil. Be sure to add sand if your soil is too heavy.

---

ILLUSTRATOR:

# Stéphanie Schouvey

**FRANCE**
@LEMONSCARLETGALERIE

**Stéphanie grew up in the south of France surrounded by rose bushes and citrus trees. She likes to paint plants after a period of sustained, patient looking. When collecting flowers, she photographs them to freeze them in a moment in time, so she can draw them whatever the time of year.**

Carole: Which medium did you use for this illustration?
Stéphanie: I used watercolour, just as botanists traditionally often did in their herbals (illustrated books that informed the reader about plants and their medicinal properties). It's a technique that's at once artistic and scientific, allowing the artist to draw a flower with both finesse and realism. I lay down successive washes or glazes of colour both on wet and dry paper.

Carole: What do you like about the peony?
Stéphanie: The peony has fascinated Chinese painters since ancient times. Its enormous, showy flowers in pinks, reds and salmons are as pretty as they come. To paint it in full bloom, almost carnal in its beauty, is to come face to face with its beating heart of stamens as if it is offering itself to the insects. In the miniature world of insects, the peony is a kind of paradise.

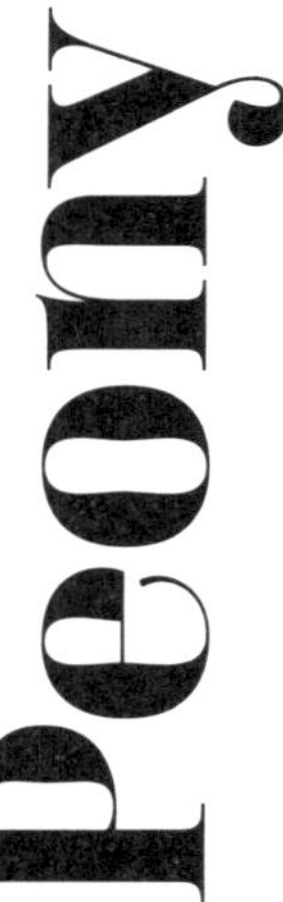

*If Stéphanie were a flower, she would be **a little climbing rose** growing against the wall of an old house, or **an anemone** with long winding stems.*

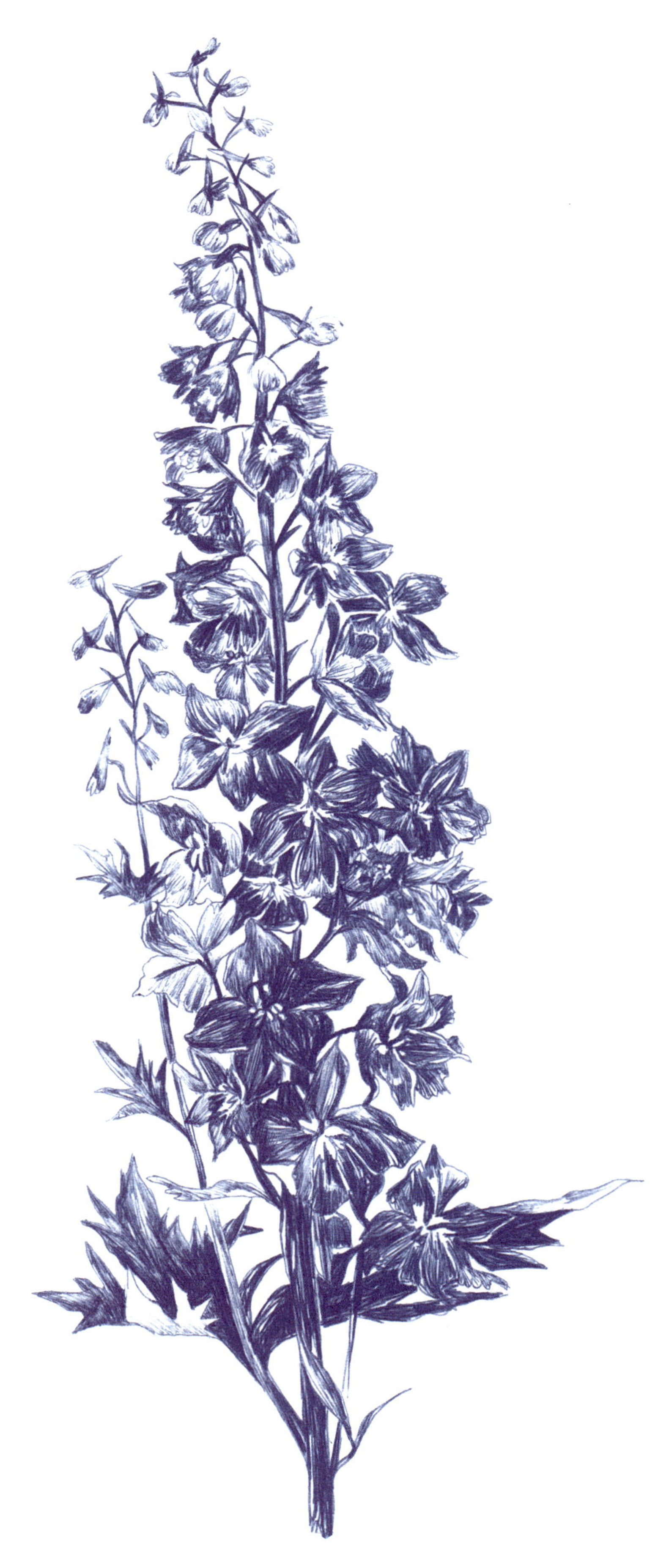

# Delphinium

**D**elphiniums are extremely visual plants. They add a strong vertical dimension to a garden, acting as an impactful yet chic visual break in the planting. Larkspur, as this flower is also known as, is often found in flower meadows and English cottage gardens.

This perennial plant likes full sun or semi-shade and a well-drained, humus-rich soil. The flower spikes (clusters growing from the main stem) can reach 2m (6½ft), so it is recommended to stake these tall, fragile stems so they don't lean or fall over.

*Please note:* every part of the delphinium is toxic. It must not be ingested, and it can irritate the skin. It's best to plant it so that pets and children can be kept out of its way – butterflies, who love feeding on its nectar, will be all the more grateful to you.

There are more than 30 species of delphinium found across the globe. The shape and colour of the flowers and leaves vary – blue, pink, red, violet and white flowers are all found. When making them into a bouquet, protect your hands, and avoid coming into contact with the sap. Cut your blooms early in the morning and quickly place your stems in fresh water.

These tips will help you keep your cut flowers for longer, as, once cut, delphiniums have a relatively short lifespan. It is better to admire them in the garden or, indeed, inside a picture frame … perhaps in the form of this illustration by Manon Cardin!

---

ILLUSTRATOR:

# Manon Cardin

**FRANCE**
@MANONCARDIN_ILLUSTRATIONS

**Manon lives in the Paris region. When she's not drawing on paper, she paints on glass or does textile design. She takes inspiration from the plants in her garden, loving their colours, surprising details and magical fragrances. Here she has caught the delphinium with nothing more than a blue biro … and her enormous talent. It's a fantastic idea, as we so often think of the colour blue when this plant comes to mind. This is a deft celebration of the star of the English country garden.**

Carole: Would you say that this is a hard flower to depict?
Manon: At first, I was a little nonplussed by its rigidity and height, but in the end I found it quite easy and pleasant to draw.

Carole: What do you like about the delphinium?
Manon: I particularly like its abundant clusters of flowers and the shape of the petals. But every flower can inspire an artwork, and I adore the idea that artists have been connected to them since the beginning of time.

*If Manon were a flower, she would be **a Paris daisy**: a wild, hardy flower of the fields, the flower of summer!*

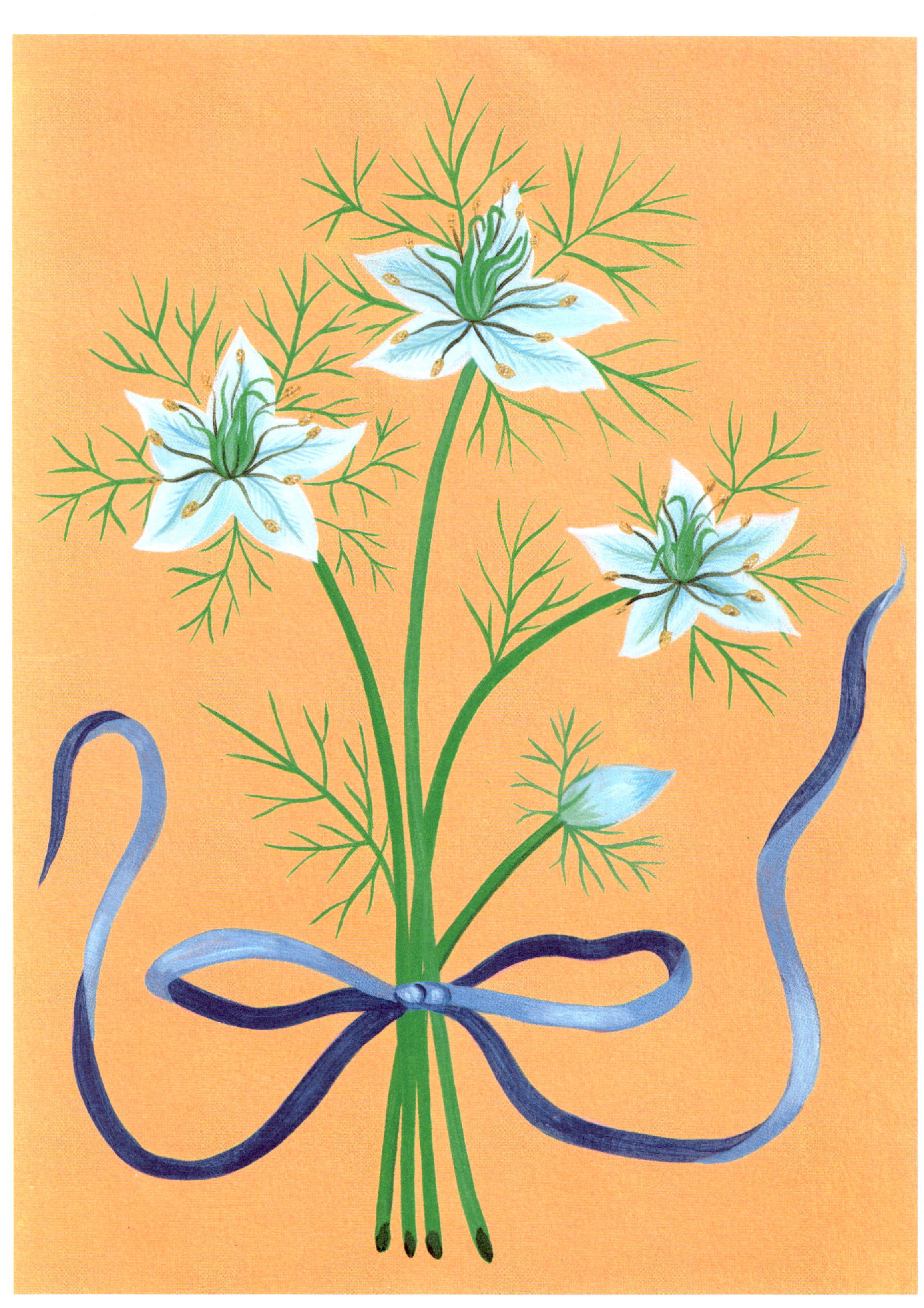

# Nigella

**A**lthough this is a species known for its medicinal and culinary uses, nigella is no less interesting as a garden plant, in your personal haven of tranquillity. Its delicate flowers and fine, misty foliage fit in harmoniously among other plants, whether perennials or annuals.

The nigella's long, abundant flowering, lasting several weeks, will add a touch of magic to your pots and beds. It does well in well-drained soil and full sun, but also tolerates light shade. This annual self-sows thanks to its black seeds, hence its name: *niger* in Latin means 'black'. These tiny black marvels are prized for both their health and culinary properties. In phytotherapy, the pressed seeds are used to produce an oil known for its purifying, antioxidant and calming benefits. The ancient Egyptian queen Nefertiti is said to have used nigella oil to improve her skin.

This pretty plant can be used to make both fresh and dried bouquets. For the latter, the flowers must be dried upside down. The fruits – which take the form of globe-like capsules – look lovely, too.

When we think of nigella flowers, we immediately see them as blue, which is the most common kind. However, there are also white, pink, violet and red nigellas. The last two colours seem to emphasize the sophisticated, mysterious aspect of the plant. *Nigella damascena* is the most commonly found of the 20 species found worldwide.

ILLUSTRATOR:

# Brianda Fitz James Stuart

**SPAIN**
@BRIANDAFJSTUART

**Here, Brianda has used acrylics to emphasize the mystical charm of the nigella. I love her work which comes in the form of paintings, rugs, wallpapers and even diaries. For her, the nigella's delicate, fantastical foliage is like a network of tiny electrical currents.**

Carole: What is your creative process?
Brianda: When I paint, I prefer to begin with an image or a photograph, taken from a book or the internet. That said, I always give free rein to my imagination, and let myself be guided by the process of painting, which, as it unfolds, shows me its own paths.

Carole: Why do you think flowers are such a source of inspiration?
Brianda: I am on an endless quest to uncover beauty, which is the leitmotif of my work … and there is nothing more beautiful than nature, of which flowers are the ultimate celebratory expression.

*If Brianda were a flower, she would be **a lotus** … a symbol of purity, resilience and spirituality – qualities that echo her own deep quest for beauty.*

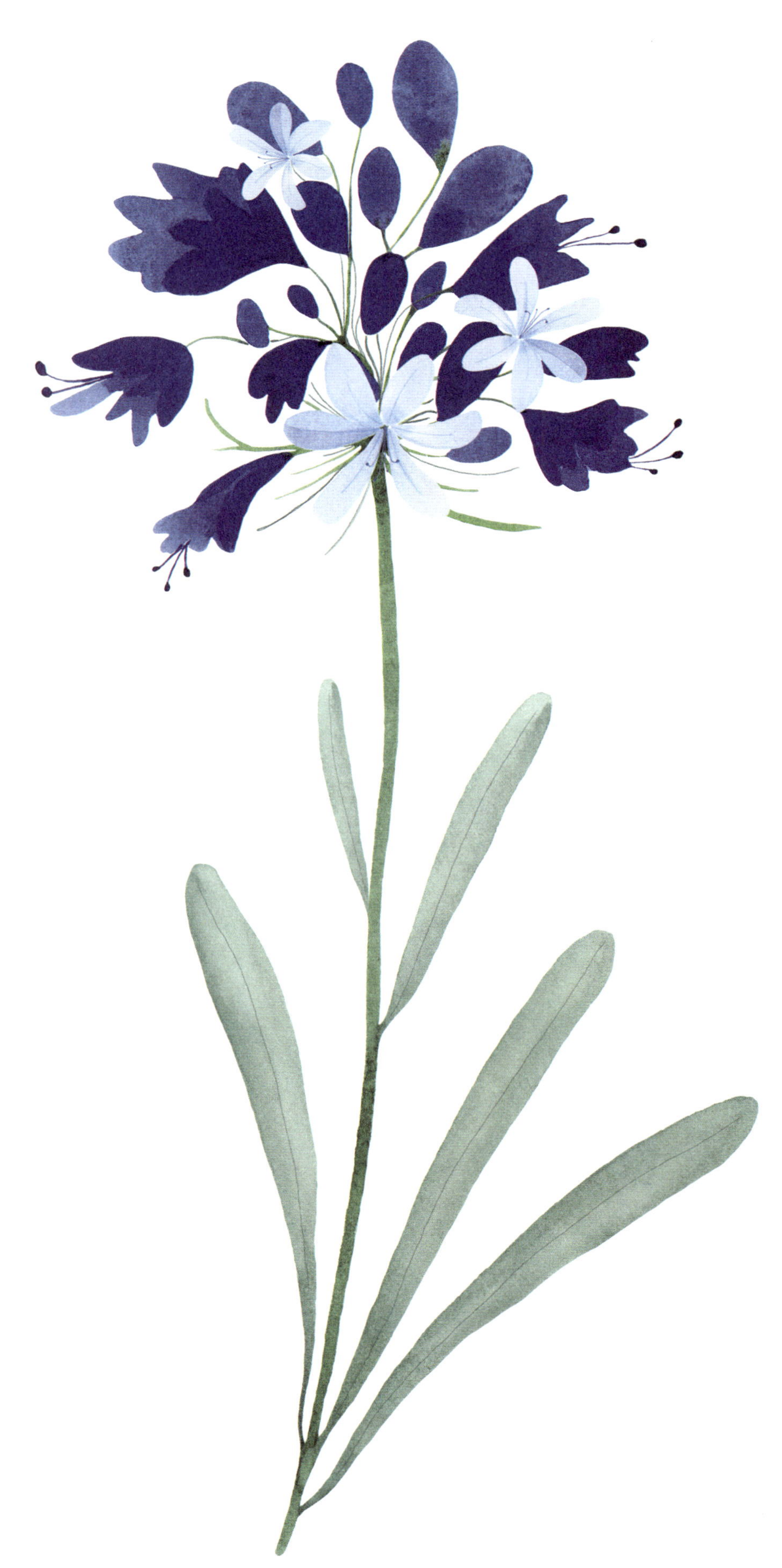

AGAPANTHUS
OR LILY OF THE NILE

**BOTANICAL FAMILY:**
AMARYLLIDACEAE.

**BLOOMS:**
JULY–AUGUST.

**WHEN TO PLANT:**
MARCH–APRIL.

**COLOURS:**
BLUE OR WHITE.

# Agapanthus

**F**or me, agapanthus flowers symbolize my parents' house in the south of France. Behind the house, where the garden is, frankly, less lovely, they stand erect like proud, majestic queens, ready to defy the winds. I've always been seduced by their shade of blue, their haughty manner and their graphic quality whose secret only nature knows. The other asset of the agapanthus is their dense, ribbon-like foliage. It can also be a useful plant for apprentice garden designers who want to create eye-catching beds or borders. What's more, some varieties are evergreen.

Agapanthuses are generally planted in spring in well-drained, fertile soil. If your soil is too heavy, lighten it using pozzolan, gravel, compost or leafmould. This perennial, which can also be grown in pots, has trouble flowering in clay soils. It is recommended that you dig a hole twice as large as the root ball. Once planted, make sure that the root crown – the area where stem and root meet – is at the soil line. Space your plants every 50cm (20in).

Note that the agapanthus needs at least a few hours of direct sun every day. The flower stems turn towards the sun, which is what keeps them upright.

Water agapanthus plants regularly but not too much, as the roots are prone to rot. In winter, cover them with garden fleece.

Fussy about water, sun loving, and in need of a good winter coat? Yes, the agapanthus is undoubtedly the prima donna of the garden!

ILLUSTRATOR:

# Annabelle Ruchat

**FRANCE**
@ANNA_ILLUSTRATIONS

**Some of the greatest painters have chosen the agapanthus as their muse. Stylistically highly interesting, the agapanthus becomes, in response to Annabelle's brush, an ethereal, resplendent beauty. In this beautiful tribute, her medium of choice – watercolour – enables the artist to bring out both the flower's graphic simplicity and subtle tones.**

**Carole:** How did you go about this design?

**Annabelle:** I often go to the Cherbourg Peninsula where the agapanthus grows in abundance, both in gardens and beside roads and railway tracks. Seeing and admiring them so often, they have imprinted themselves onto my mind. But my memory has transformed them. This isn't a faithful rendition of the flower.

**Carole:** Why do flowers inspire so many artists?
**Annabelle:** Because they prove that perfection exists!

*If Annabelle were a flower, she would be **a yellow rudbeckia** splattering the world with sunshine and joy.*

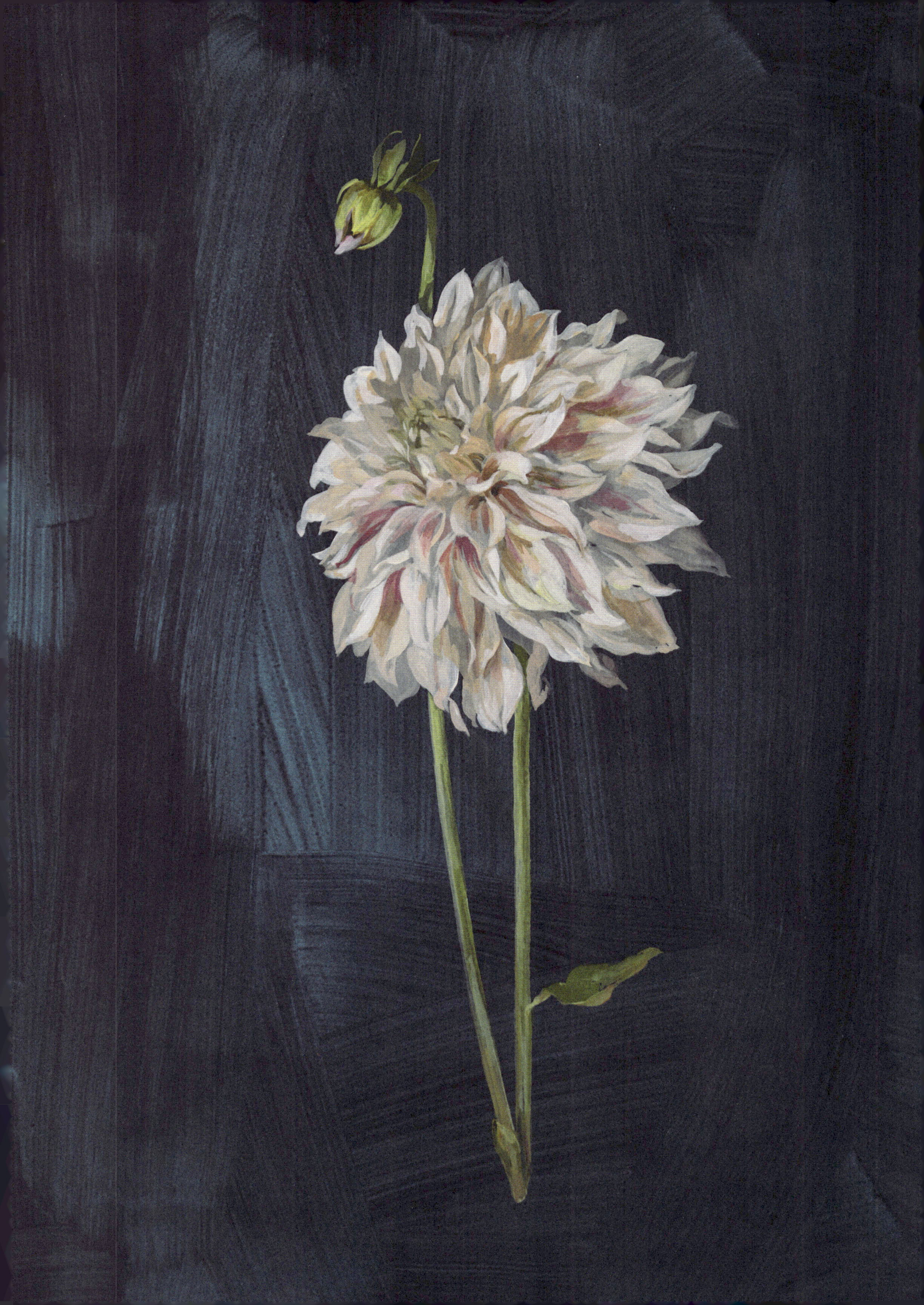

## Dahlia

DAHLIA

**BOTANICAL FAMILY:**
ASTERACEAE.

**BLOOMS:**
JUNE–NOVEMBER.

**WHEN TO PLANT:**
MARCH–APRIL
(IN WARMER REGIONS).
MAY
(IN COOLER REGIONS).

**COLOURS:**
RED, WHITE, PEACH, ORANGE, YELLOW, PINK, VIOLET, PURPLE, BICOLOURED.

I think I fell in love with dahlias while doing a report on the Parc floral de Paris for the French gardening programme *Silence, ça pousse!* For 30 years the City of Paris has organized an international dahlia competition encompassing varieties from all over the world. Every producer sends their flowers to the competition, so you are really lost as to where to look first. Having been repeatedly hybridized, the dahlia offers a range of possibilities.

Here are a few of my own favourites:
• 'Lakeview Peach Fuzz' for its tones of apricot
• The giant 'Café au Lait', often used at weddings
• The lovely 'Arabian Night' in deep Bordeaux red.

The dahlia owes its name to the Swedish botanist Anders Dahl (1751–89), who introduced it into Europe in 1789. Native to Mexico, dahlias are extremely sensitive to the cold. You should wait until the soil reaches at least 15°C before planting, ideally two weeks after the last spring frosts. As you might expect, these tender plants need full sunshine. Consider staking the biggest varieties, which can grow as tall as 1.5m (5ft); the smallest reach only 30cm (12in). When winter comes, my advice is to dig up the tubers and store them in a dry place between 4 and 10°C.

I find it funny that for a long time dahlias were considered the old-fashioned granny of the plant world. No longer! So perhaps even the geranium has every chance of enjoying a revival in a few years' time …

ILLUSTRATOR:

# Flora Roberts

**UNITED KINGDOM**
@FLORA.ROBERTS

Born in Scotland but now living in the English county of Dorset, Flora Roberts loves to be surrounded by nature. She creates her work by observing the changing seasons, taking inspiration from her own garden or else from Dutch 17th-century still lifes.

**Carole:** How did you reproduce the dahlia on paper?
**Flora:** Dahlias are a real challenge because they have so many petals arranged in such a complicated pattern, but it's a *good* challenge. I decided to use highly pigmented watercolours to bring the flowers to life – flowers I find joyous and sometimes even a little bit whimsical.

**Carole:** What do flowers evoke for you in general?
**Flora:** They have so much character, and I think of them as taking up poses like dancers. I like to follow and paint them across the seasons.

*If Flora were a flower, she would be **a rose** – the beauty queen of the garden.*

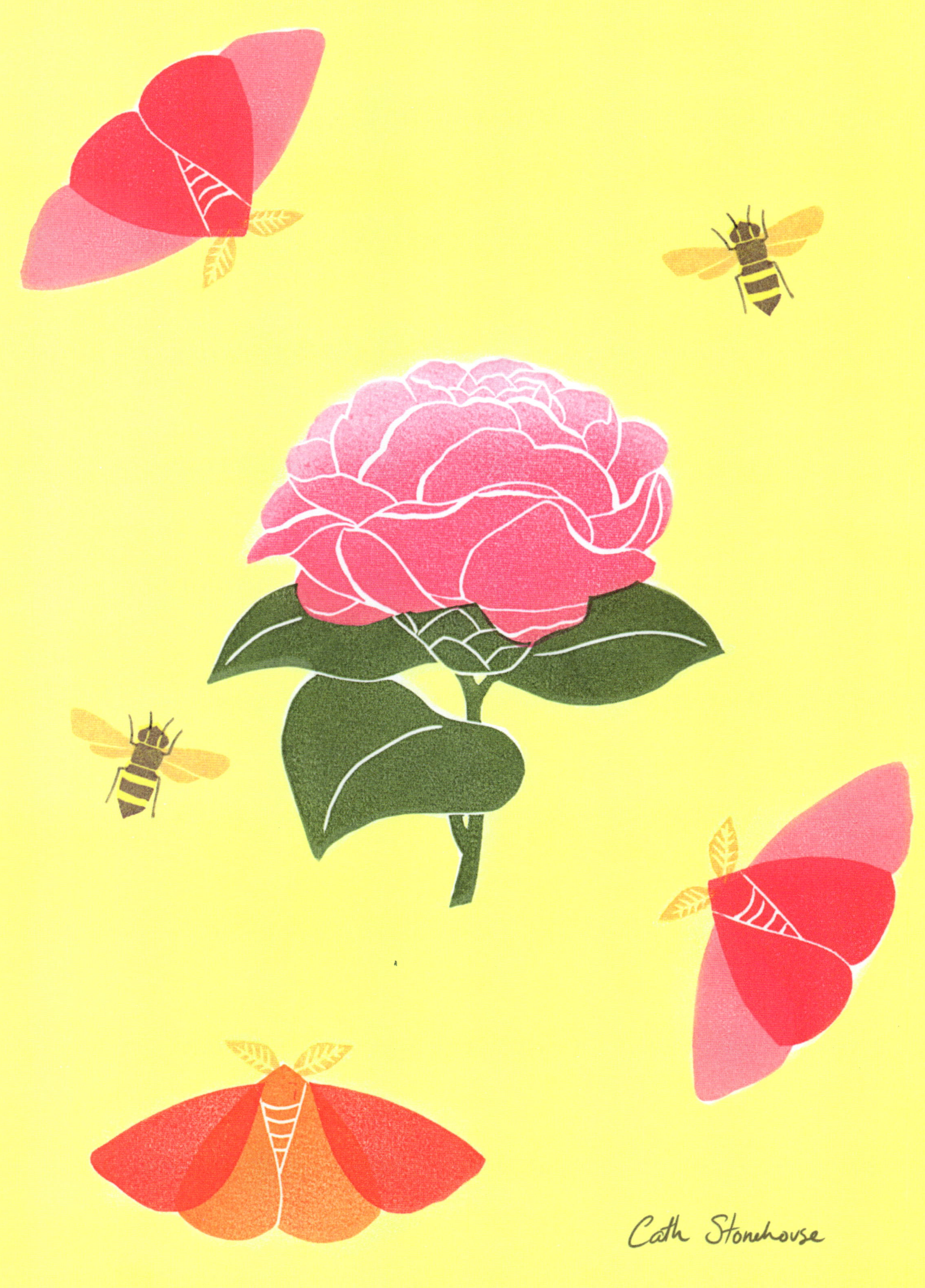

Cath Stonehouse

# Camellia

**T**he introduction of this shrub into Europe is linked to that of tea a century and a half earlier. Camellias, which arrived in London at the end of the 18th century, disappointed many English people as they had been expecting tea trees. Whether through a mistaken seed purchase or a deliberate act of subterfuge on the part of the Chinese as they sought to protect their economic heritage, the history of camellias in the West had begun.

Thousands of varieties exist today, the best known being the Japanese camellia, with its delicate flowerheads nestled among dark-green, shiny leaves. Rather less conventional is the 'Sanpei-tsubaki', a variety that produces smaller but highly original flowers. My advice is to plant both a spring- and autumn-flowering camellia to prolong the pleasure provided by its blooms. Among those that bloom into winter is the *Camellia sasanqua* 'Early Pearly', with its double flowers the colour of mother-of-pearl. It is hardy, evergreen and splendid for a romantic garden, as well as easy to maintain. Camellias like well-drained, somewhat acidic soils. My camellia grows next to a heather, and they make perfect companions. Choose a site in indirect sun or light shade sheltered from cold winds.

I can't end these brief lines on the camellia without referring to Alexandre Dumas *fils* (1824–95) whose novel *The Lady of the Camellias* (1848) was inspired by the life of a famous 19th-century courtesan, Marie Duplessis. I first read this story of passion and impossible love in my adolescence, and it has haunted me ever since.

ILLUSTRATOR:

# Catherine Stonehouse

**SPAIN**
@CATH_STONEHOUSE

**Catherine is an Australian who today lives in a village in north-east Spain. Pine forests, wildflowers and the Mediterranean Sea provide the perfect setting for creativity.**

**Carole:** Can you say something about your creative process?
**Catherine:** My linocuts of flowers are always based on drawings. I love drawing flowers and try to do so on a regular basis (every morning!). Here I've chosen to go for block printing. Each colour is an individually sculpted block that interlinks with the other colour blocks. It's a new way of lino printing which brings greater versatility because you can very easily modify the composition.

**Carole:** Why are flowers so omnipresent in your work?
**Catherine:** For me, flowers always stand for sensuality, love and joy. In terms of the camellia, I like how the tender pinks of the blooms contrast with the deep-green of the leaves, and how the petals are so delicate and gentle.

*If Catherine were a flower, she would be **a geranium** for its luminosity and the fact that it flourishes in windowboxes – bringing joy to everyday life!*

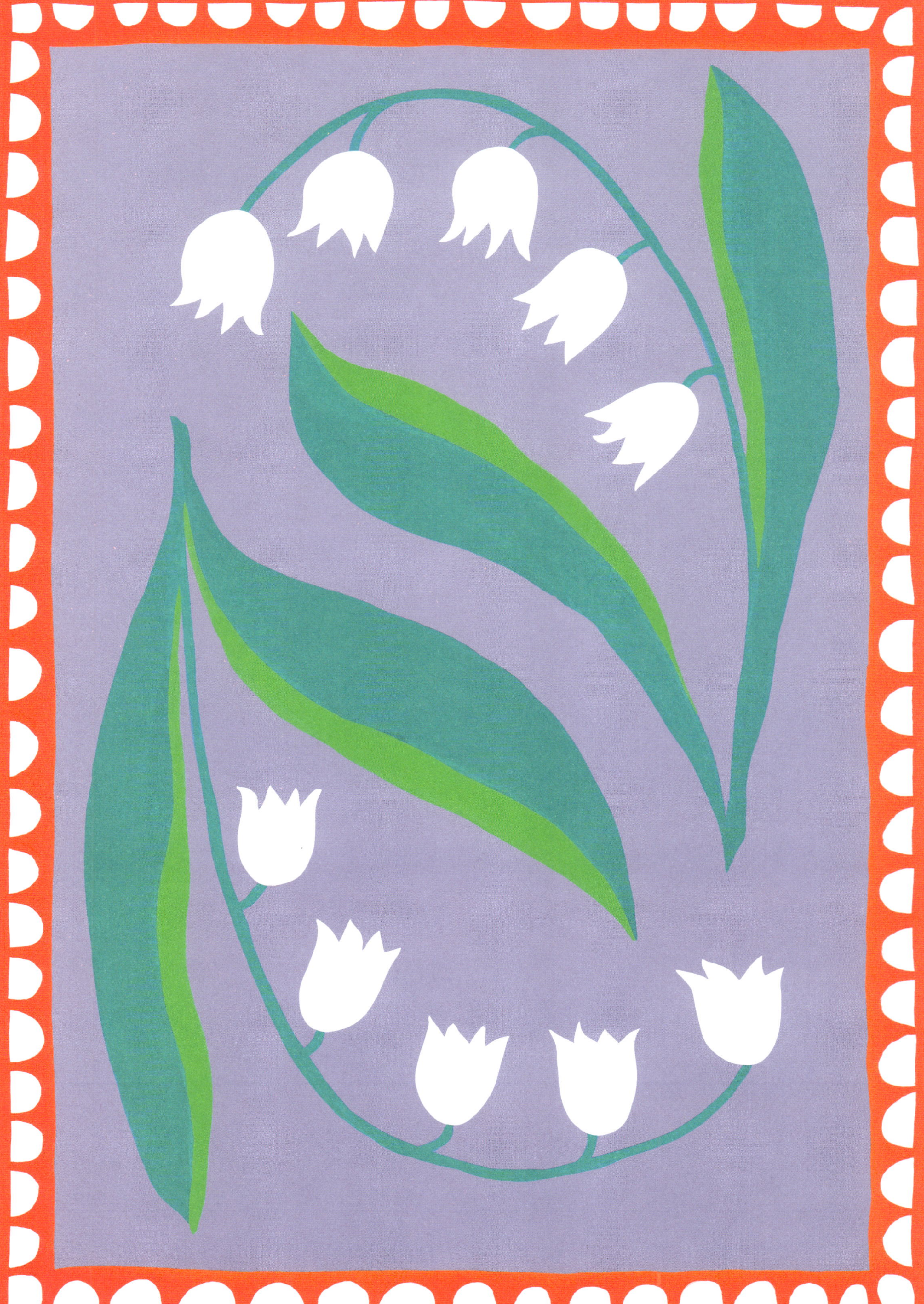

LILY OF THE VALLEY
OR MAY BELLS

---

**BOTANICAL
FAMILY:**
ASPARAGACEAE.

---

**BLOOMS:**
APRIL–MAY.

---

**WHEN TO PLANT:**
MARCH AND OCTOBER.

---

**COLOURS:**
WHITE, PINK, RED.

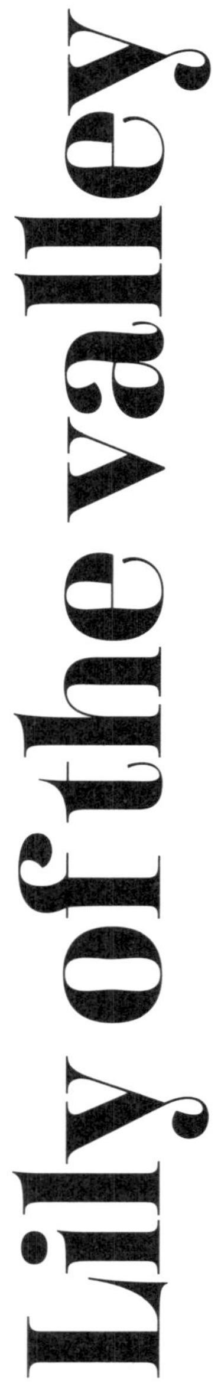


**T**his is a plant which causes a stir not so much for its pretty white bells but its history. In one popular French tradition, on May Day, people exchange sprigs of lily of the valley as a token of friendship, prosperity and the beginning of spring.

Native across northern Eurasia (except in Ireland), the plant has been grown in Europe since the Middle Ages, when it was a symbol of love. In May – the traditional month for weddings – it was the custom to hang a bouquet of the flowers on the door of the bride-to-be as a symbol of her purity. At this time, in France, another word for 'to flirt' was *mugueter* – from the French word for the flower, *muguet*. In the town of Helston, in Cornwall, the flower is worn on Floral Day – the 8th of May.

For all its loveliness, delicate fragrance and associations with happiness, the lily of the valley is toxic and invasive. It likes semi-shade and humus-rich soils. We think of it as having exclusively white flowers, but there are red and pink varieties, too.

My research into the flower revealed that the couturier Christian Dior always carried a dried sprig of lily of valley about with him and even had sprigs sewn into the lining of the runway clothes at his fashion shows. If you, too, are a superstitious fashion designer, perhaps you should do the same!

---

ILLUSTRATOR:

# Adeline Chemin

**FRANCE**
@ADELINECHEMIN

**An illustrator and art workshop leader, Adeline adores sharing her passion with others. For this illustration, she has used gouache – an opaque water-based paint that offers both a rich texture and a vibrant, luminous colour.**

Carole: Is it tricky to reproduce the lily of the valley?
Adeline: The flower can be painstaking to draw because of its distinctively shaped bells. So I'd say yes, if your goal is to reproduce it identically. But what I prefer to do in my own work is to simplify the shapes so as to create an image that evokes the flower and captures its essence. This is the reason why the work on the composition and the colours is extremely important.

Carole: What do you like about this flower?
Adeline: When I see its little white bells beginning to bud, I know that spring has arrived. I also appreciate the May Day traditions and the notion that this flower brings happiness and luck to those who receive it. It's a simple gesture but one laden with meaning. What's more, its delicate fragrance is intoxicating.

*If Adeline were a flower, she would be **a pansy** because this perennial suits her introspective nature. Also for its unbelievable shades of violet, a colour dear to this artist.*

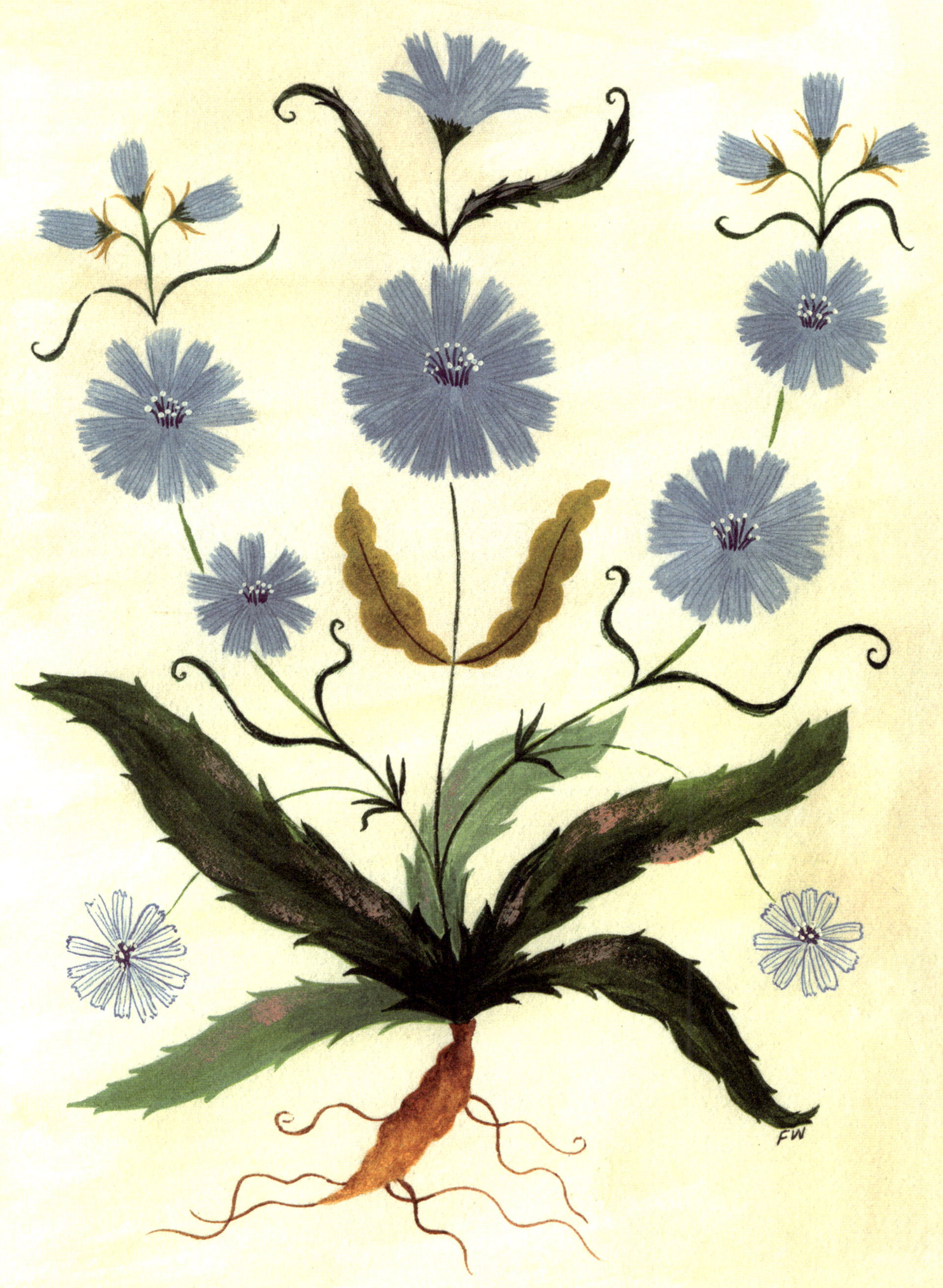

**BOTANICAL
FAMILY:**
ASTERACEAE.

**BLOOMS:**
MAY—SEPTEMBER.

**WHEN TO PLANT:**
AS SEEDLINGS IN MAY
AND AUGUST.

**COLOURS:**
BLUE, SOMETIMES
PINK OR WHITE.

# Wild chicory

**D**o you prefer your wild chicory in a salad, in a bouquet or inside a picture frame? For me, this biennial plant is a visual feast. For starters, just look at its toothed leaves that look very much like the dandelion's – though with one big difference: their undersides are hairy! To eat them, harvest the leaves from February, blanch them to reduce their bitterness, and mix them with other salad leaves. You can also mix them, raw or cooked, with other vegetables, serve them alongside a cheese selection, or dry them and infuse them in hot water to make the well-known 'chicory coffee'.

Wild chicory flowers have a simple, natural beauty. The flower heads open up with the first rays of the sun, revealing slender, lightly toothed petals in vibrant azure blue. This spectacle is best caught by early birds as the flower begins to fade through the day before finally closing again.

In its wild state, it is found in meadows, on roadsides and in neglected patches of land. But there is nothing to stop you growing it in your garden to provide a splash of sky blue in a border or to brighten up your vegetable patch. Chicory appreciates full sun and a well-drained, slightly alkaline soil in which to anchor its taproot.

---

ILLUSTRATOR:

# Flora Waycott

**AUSTRALIA**
@FLORAWAYCOTT

**Flora is a British artist living in Australia whose works in gouache are an ode to nature, plants and everyday objects. Look closely at her art and you will appreciate all the finesse and delicacy of her work. Here she has focused almost entirely on the flower head, with the edges of the petals resembling pretty eyelashes, each one carefully delineated.**

Carole: Could you describe your creative process?
Flora: I used English Breakfast tea to tint the background of the paper, giving the image a soft, aged look. I then painted the flowers in gouache with lots of water to emphasize their fragility. A blend of greens gives the leaves depth, and pale-pink highlights bring light and movement to the whole.

Carole: How would you describe your relationship with flowers?
Flora: Flowers play an important role in my life, and I turn to them in all sorts of emotional situations. They hold memories and are a source of optimism. Their colours, tints and details inspire me in my art practice. I also like to think that my relationship with them is linked to my first name, as if the flowers know that I am one of them.

*If Flora were a flower, she would be **the paintbrush lily** – for its unique and spectacular orange bloom. 'It's a plant', says Flora, 'that saves up its energy for a brief moment of splendour.'*

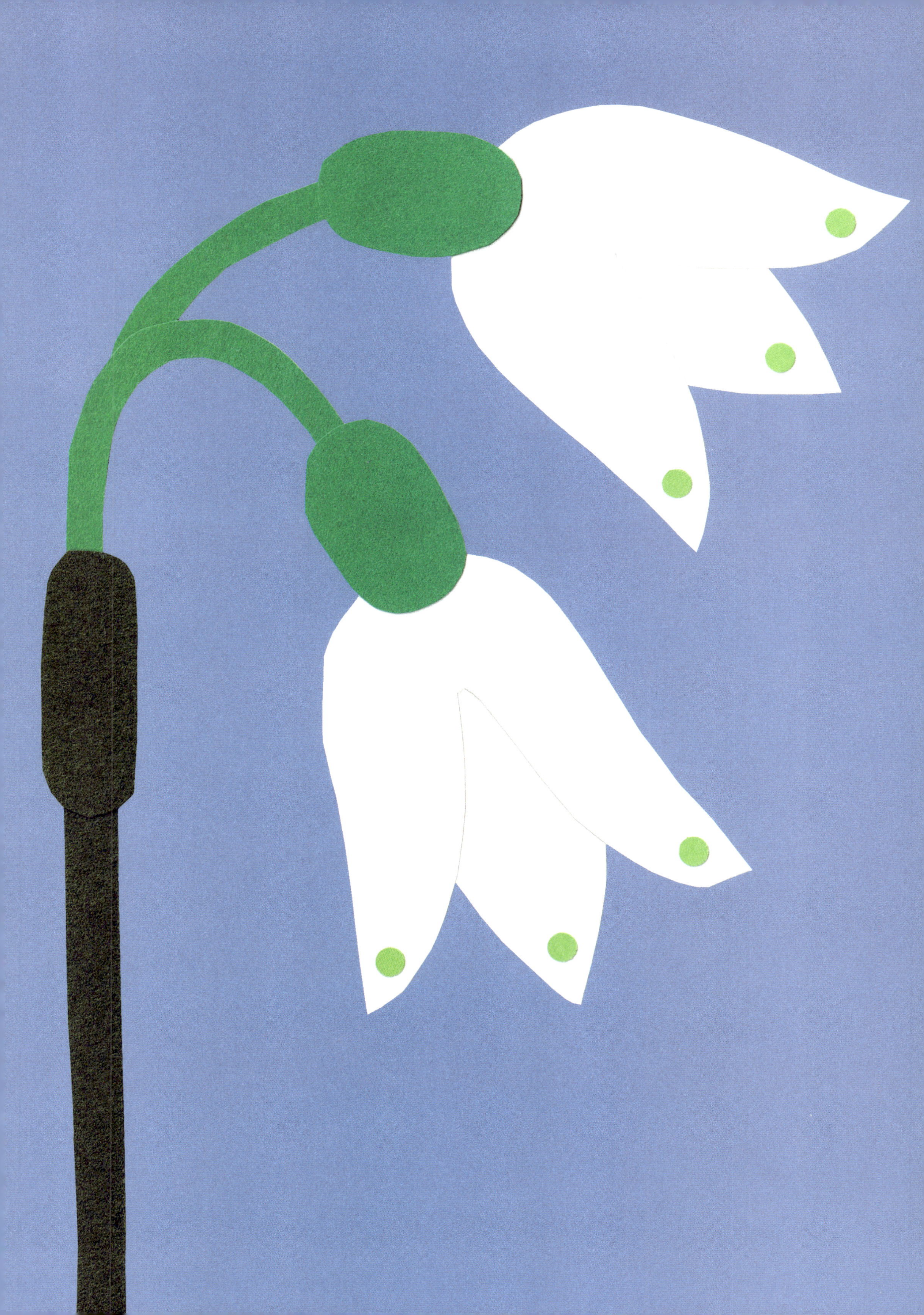

**T**he snowdrop is the elegant alarm clock of the fields and of sleeping gardens. It pierces through the winter snows – hence its French name, *perce-neige* – to astonish us with its immaculate white bells. It symbolizes the much anticipated arrival of spring and the rebirth of flowers. With its three large sepals and three much smaller petals, the snowdrop droops its head as if out of shyness, even though it seems so valiant. Every year it's a heart-warming delight when I first spot it in Stéphane Marie's garden, during shoots for the French gardening programme *Silence, ça pousse!*

To enjoy the snowdrop in your garden, plant the bulbs in autumn. They need a well-drained soil – too wet and the bulbs may rot. Dig 5–8cm (2–3½in)-deep holes, 10cm (4in) apart. Soak the bulbs and then plant them with the pointed end facing upwards.

The snowdrop likes cool, humus-rich soil in full sun or semi-shade. After a few years, the bulbs multiply and the plants form ever-denser clumps. At the end of summer, you can dig them up, separate them out and replant them farther apart. *Note:* it's recommended that you wear gloves when handling the bulbs as they are toxic and can irritate the skin.

The snowdrop, with its flower spike and long, slender leaves is the cutie of nature and was much loved by the artists of Art Nouveau. The snowdrop, as it happens, offers the perfect silhouette for a lamp!

---

ILLUSTRATOR:

# Maki Toy

**SOUTH KOREA**
@MAKITOY

**Luckily, Maki Toy lives a long way away from me as otherwise I would be forever visiting her! I would start by rifling through the many carefully numbered notebooks and sketchbooks arranged on her shelves. I love not only her creative method but also the way she composes her colours.**

Carole: Could you explain your work process for this illustration?
Maki Toy: The snowdrop has a rather simple shape but I particularly love one detail: the end points of its petals. When I begin a design, I give myself permission to simplify the general shape. I sketch this out on coloured papers then take out my scissors and my glue and move on to the composition.

Carole: In what way is nature a source of inspiration for you?
Maki Toy: The diversity of shapes and colours found in plants always gives me a lot of joy. With each encounter, something magical happens and new ideas and visions unfold.

*If Maki Toy were a flower, she would be **a yellow tulip**. She has adored this graceful member of the lily family since childhood.*

Snowdrop

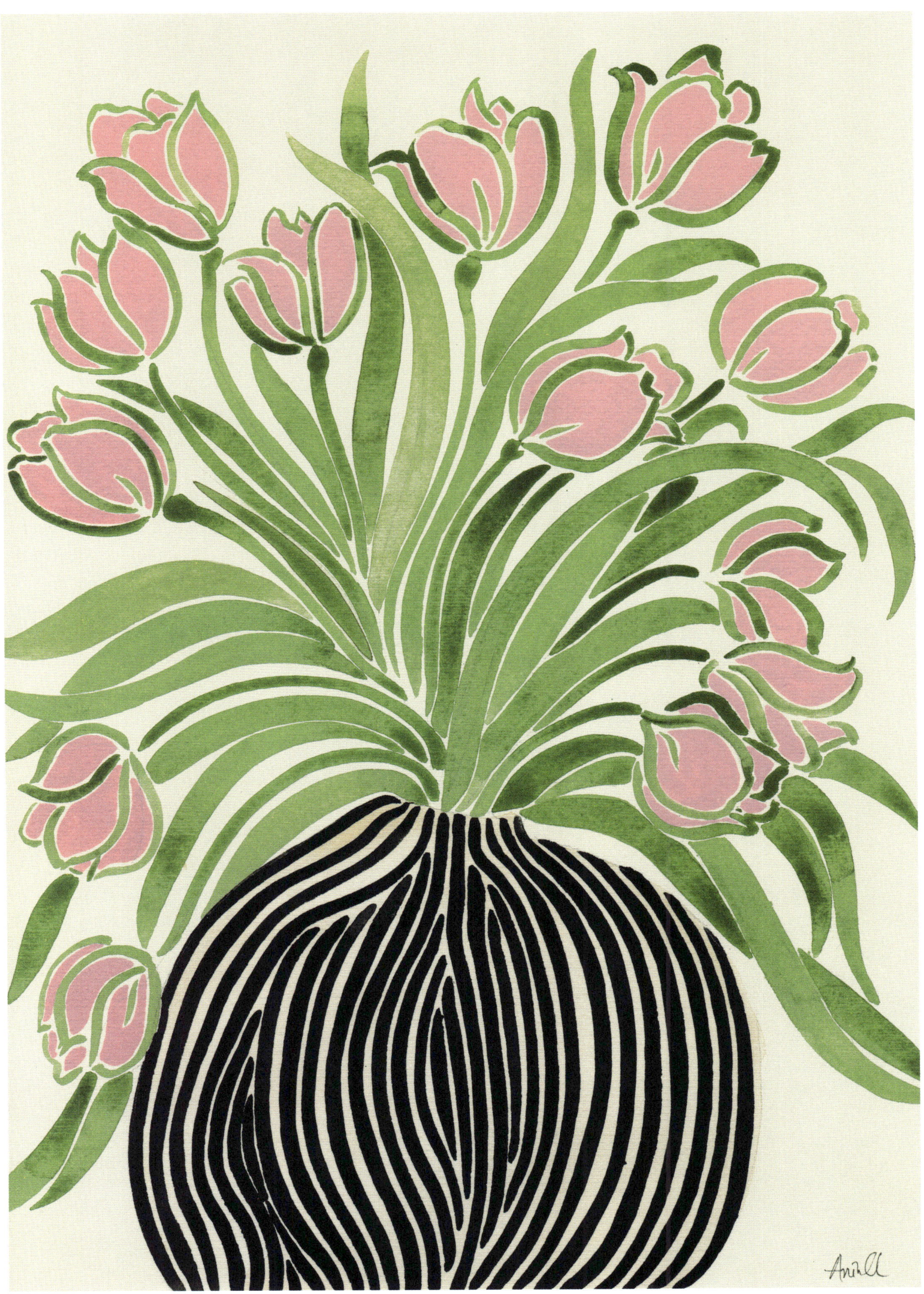
Amell

TULIP

**BOTANICAL FAMILY:**
LILIACEAE.

**BLOOMS:**
MARCH–MID-JUNE DEPENDING ON THE VARIETY.

**WHEN TO PLANT:**
SEPTEMBER–NOVEMBER.

**COLOURS:**
RED, PINK, YELLOW, WHITE, ORANGE, VIOLET, PURPLE, BICOLOUR.

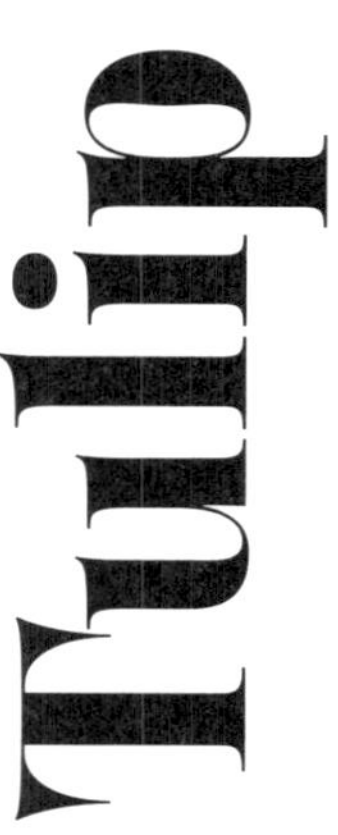

**D**ouble tulips, parrot tulips, fringed tulips, lily-flowered tulips … humanity's love for this flower has never stopped inspiring horticulturalists. Just the dream-inducing names of the thousands of varieties show this. I love the lily-flowered tulip 'Sappora', but my latest passion is for the lace-fringed tulips such as the unbelievably beautiful 'Lambada'. If you prefer to avoid the ruffled look, but want a tulip with a spark of originality, take a look at 'Happy Generation', a long-flowering Triumph tulip: this has astonishing large white petals stippled with vivid red 'flames'.

These perennial flowering bulbs need a sandy soil, which can be either acidic or alkaline as long as it is well drained. The bulbs must be planted with their pointed ends facing upwards and at a depth twice their length. Plant these beauties in drifts of at least 30, spacing each bulb 10–20cm (4–8in) apart depending on their size. Plant in areas that get full sun, as in more shady spots they will be less productive.

If you want your bulbs to reflower the following year, give them sufficient time to build up their reserves. As soon as the flower has faded, deadhead it. Then, once the foliage has turned yellow, coming up to June, dig up your bulbs and dry them in a dry, well-ventilated place, spaced out in crates filled with scrunched-up newspaper … and that's it. Replant in September, which will enable them to get established before winter sets in.

---

ILLUSTRATOR:

# Anine Cecilie Iversen

**DENMARK**
@LAPOIREIMAGINAIRE

**For this gouache and watercolour painting, Anine Cecilie has used a photograph as her source, but the vase comes straight out of her imagination.**

Carole: What piques your curiosity when it comes to tulips?
Anine Cecilie: I love their simple shapes, their vivid colours and their two long leaves. They exist in a huge number of varieties, in terms of their petals and even textures, which makes them engaging and exciting to study. The foliage gives an organic movement to the design, of which I am particularly fond.

Carole: What relationship do you have with flowers?
Anine Cecilie: I am fascinated by the teeming gamut of colours, patterns and shapes, and their ceaseless transformation during the flowering season. Painting them gives me a way to feel connected with living things. I'm always discovering fresh details, which change the way I look at flowers and surprise me at every turn. This works well with my intuitive way of painting.

*If Anine Cecilie were a flower, she would be **a peony** or, indeed, **a tulip**, for their grace and shape. They are her favourite cut flowers to have in her home.*

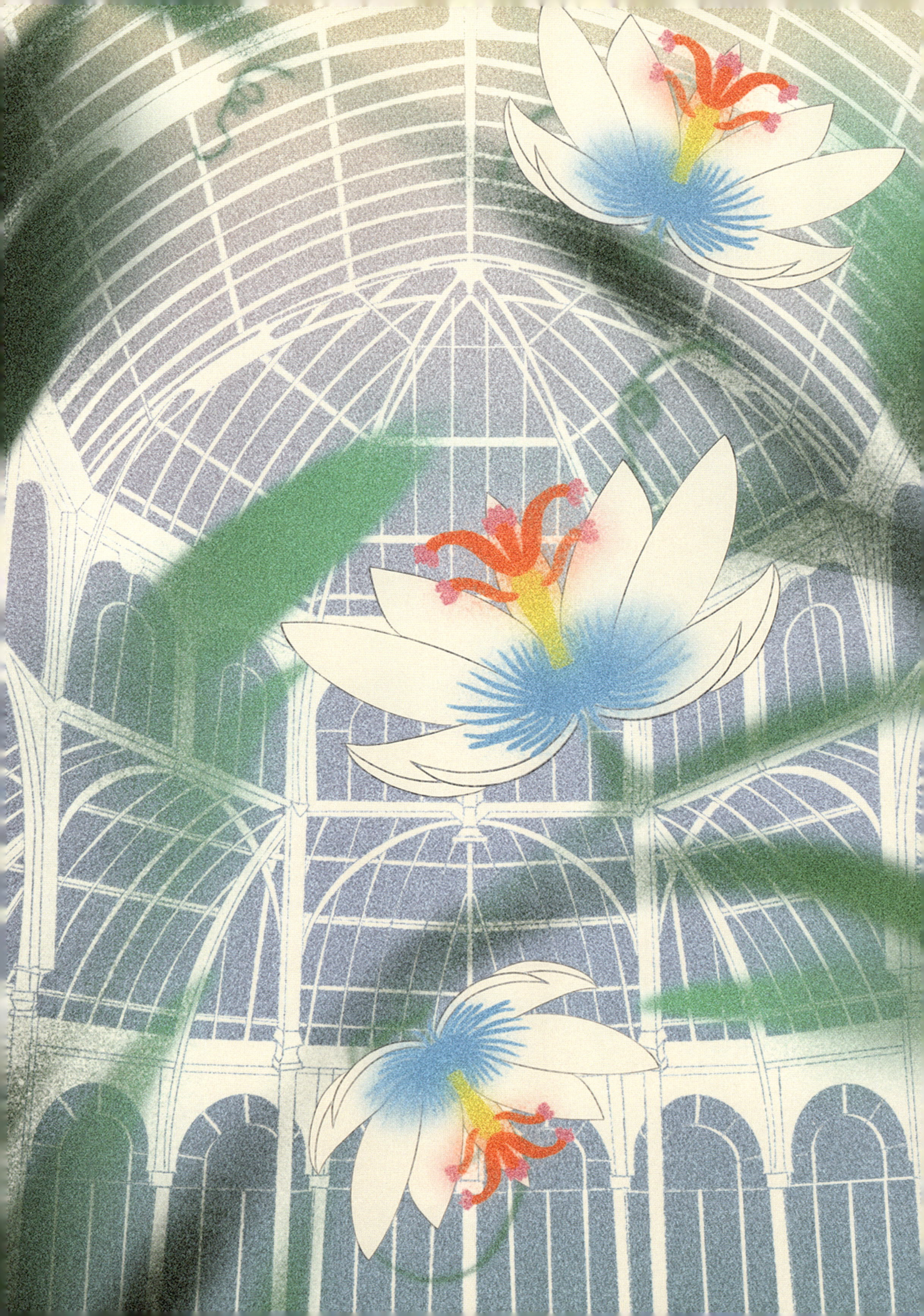

PASSION FLOWER OR
PASSIFLORA

**BOTANICAL
FLOWER:**
PASSIFLORACEAE.

**BLOOMS:**
JUNE–SEPTEMBER.

**WHEN TO PLANT:**
APRIL–SEPTEMBER.

**COLOURS:**
WHITE, PINK, RED,
BLUE, PURPLE.

# Passion flower

**With its vivid colours and graphic quality, this climbing vine brings exoticism and originality in spades to your garden. The foliage is more or less evergreen, but it is its enormous, subtly colourful flowers (8–15cm (3½–6in) in diameter) that truly astonish. The flowers have a certain pop-up quality: the sepals and petals open up in a double crown of petaloid tepals (undifferentiated petals and sepals) like something in a 3D book, offering a ravishing spectacle of projecting stamens and a pistil made up of three fleshy stigmas. These floral ornaments have long been associated with the Passion of Christ, hence the name. The five petals and five sepals represent the Apostles (excluding St Peter and Judas), the five stamens evoke the five wounds of Christ, the three stigmas of the pistil recall the three nails of the Cross, and the 72 filaments suggest the 72 thorns of the Holy Crown – I'll leave you to do the counting.**

Just like the wild chicory, the passion flower has its daily routine: the flowers open around 10am and close late afternoon. It loves to clamber along walls or over pergolas and can reach as tall as 10m (33ft), as long as the soil is sufficiently rich and well drained. If you don't have a garden, you can plant it in a big container indoors – it makes an excellent green room divider, for example. It dislikes the cold so flourishes indoors, though you should keep it away from direct heating.

On a final note, remember that the passion flower is a medicinal plant on account of its soothing and relaxing effects when drunk as a tisane.

---

ILLUSTRATOR:

# Marine Buffard

**FRANCE**
@BECOMINGAMORNINGPERSON

**Paris-based Marine is passionate about drawing, digital computing and animation. To capture the beauty of the passion flower, she sought to highlight its psychedelic aspect by digitally processing her image.**

Carole: Is the passion flower a tricky subject? Tell us how you went about this illustration …
Marine: The passion flower is always a surprising plant but easier to depict than you'd think. I created this illustration using photographs I'd taken of my own flowers that grow on my terrace in spring. Then I opted for a stylized representation by emphasizing the geometry and symmetry of the flower.

Carole: What do you like best about flowers?
Marine: I would say their decorative, organic aspect, but without overdoing that. The mixture of colours, textures and shapes offers a wonderful visual diversity.

*If Marine were a flower, she would surely be*
**a passion flower** *or* **a tulip**.

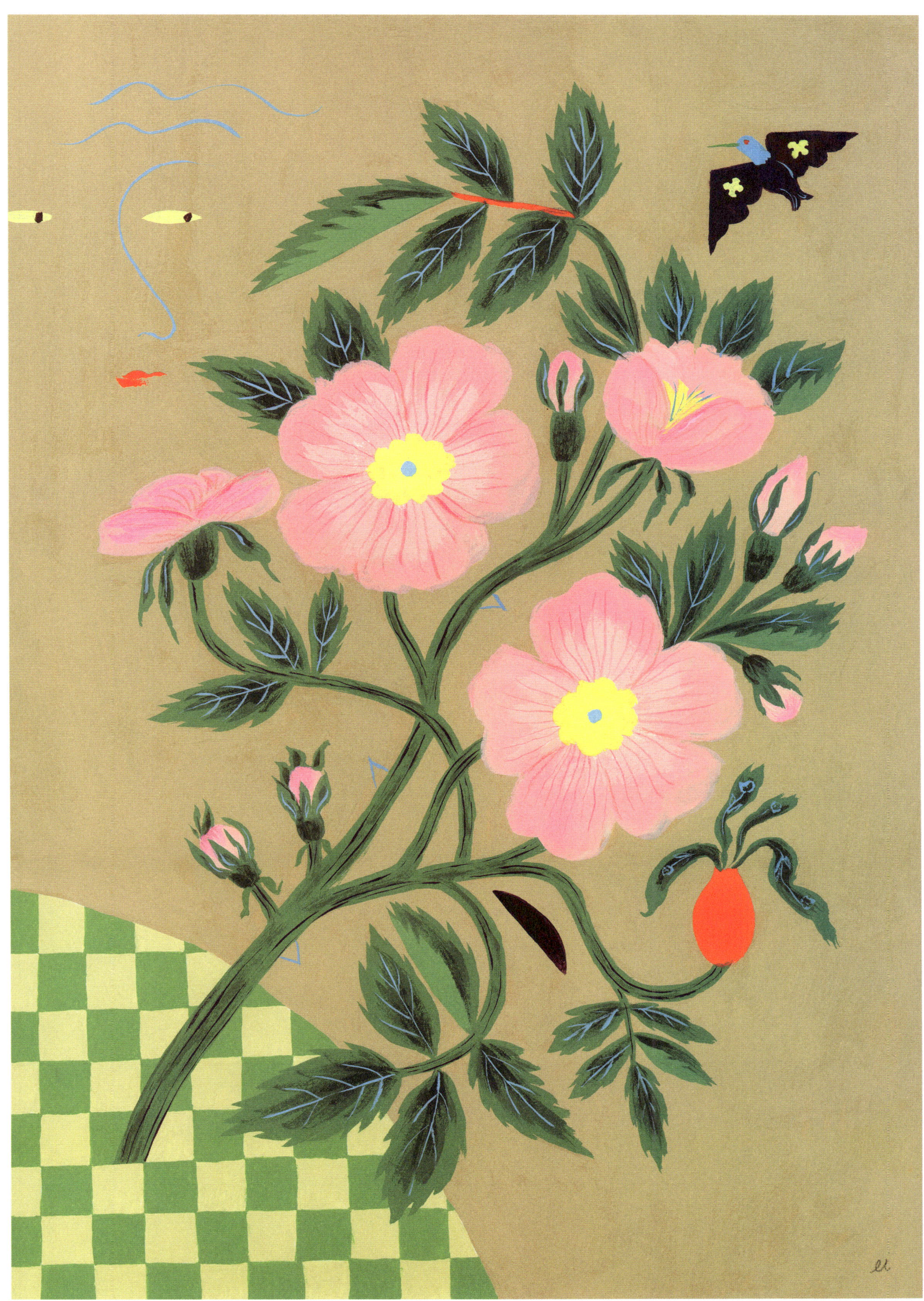

ROSE

**BOTANICAL FAMILY:**
ROSACEAE.

**BLOOMS:**
MAY–JUNE, AND
UNTIL NOVEMBER IF A
REMONTANT VARIETY.

**WHEN TO PLANT:**
MID-NOVEMBER
TO MID-MARCH.
(BARE-ROOT).

**COLOURS:**
PINK, WHITE,
RED, YELLOW,
VIOLET, PURPLE,
MULTICOLOURED.

# Rose

**W**ith some 20,000 horticultural varieties and 350 wild species, the rose would require a lifetime to study … but among this plethora there is one that means a lot to me: the 'Thelma' rose. When I first joined the TV programme *Silence, ça pousse!* , a very lovely couple who ran a family nursery in Anjou contacted me to propose naming a rose after me. I asked them to name it instead after my newborn daughter. I love to think how the 'Thelma' rose might be bringing joy to gardeners.

When planting roses it's best to buy bare-rooted plants to avoid transplant shock. Choose a position in full sunshine. Roses can deal with any soil as long as it is well balanced and well drained.

For example, a clay soil needs to be lightened with the addition of compost or manure. Water roses regularly, especially during dry spells, but avoid wetting the leaves as this can cause fungal diseases; instead, aim your watering can at the base of the plant.

English roses, rose bushes, dwarf roses or – my favourite – climbing roses are all 'queens' of the garden. Since ancient times the rose has been known as the 'eternal flower' and has been grown, bred and hybridized for its beauty and fragrance. If you love roses, respect their flowering period and gift them in summer, rather than as a Saint Valentine's Day love token. In February, roses are grown in Dutch hothouses or imported from the ends of the earth. By gifting roses when they are in season, you will show your love for our planet.

ILLUSTRATOR:

# Emily Isabella

**UNITED STATES**
@EMILYISABELLA

**Based in the Hudson Valley, Emily is a textile designer and illustrator. For this queen of the garden, immortalized in the book plates of the painter-cum-botanist Pierre-Joseph Redouté (1759–1840), the artist has sought to surprise her viewers by modernizing the rose. Emily has got out her gouaches, her pencils, her colours … and all her talent.**

**Carole:** Was the rose difficult to depict? How did you set about the process?
**Emily:** I confess that I find every flower hard to paint. After all, it's impossible to make them more beautiful than they already are in nature. For this image, I blended several photographs with my imagination while taking inspiration from the Molly Drake song 'Fine Summer Morning'!

**Carole:** What do you like about this flower?
**Emily:** Years ago, during a trip to Maine, I was enchanted by the beach rose (*Rosa rugosa*) and have never forgotten it. These wild flowers that grow close to the ocean really got inside me. Bright red is a colour I have always been drawn to in my work.

*If Emily were a flower, she would be **a wildflower** in a meadow, for its simple poetry and natural beauty.*

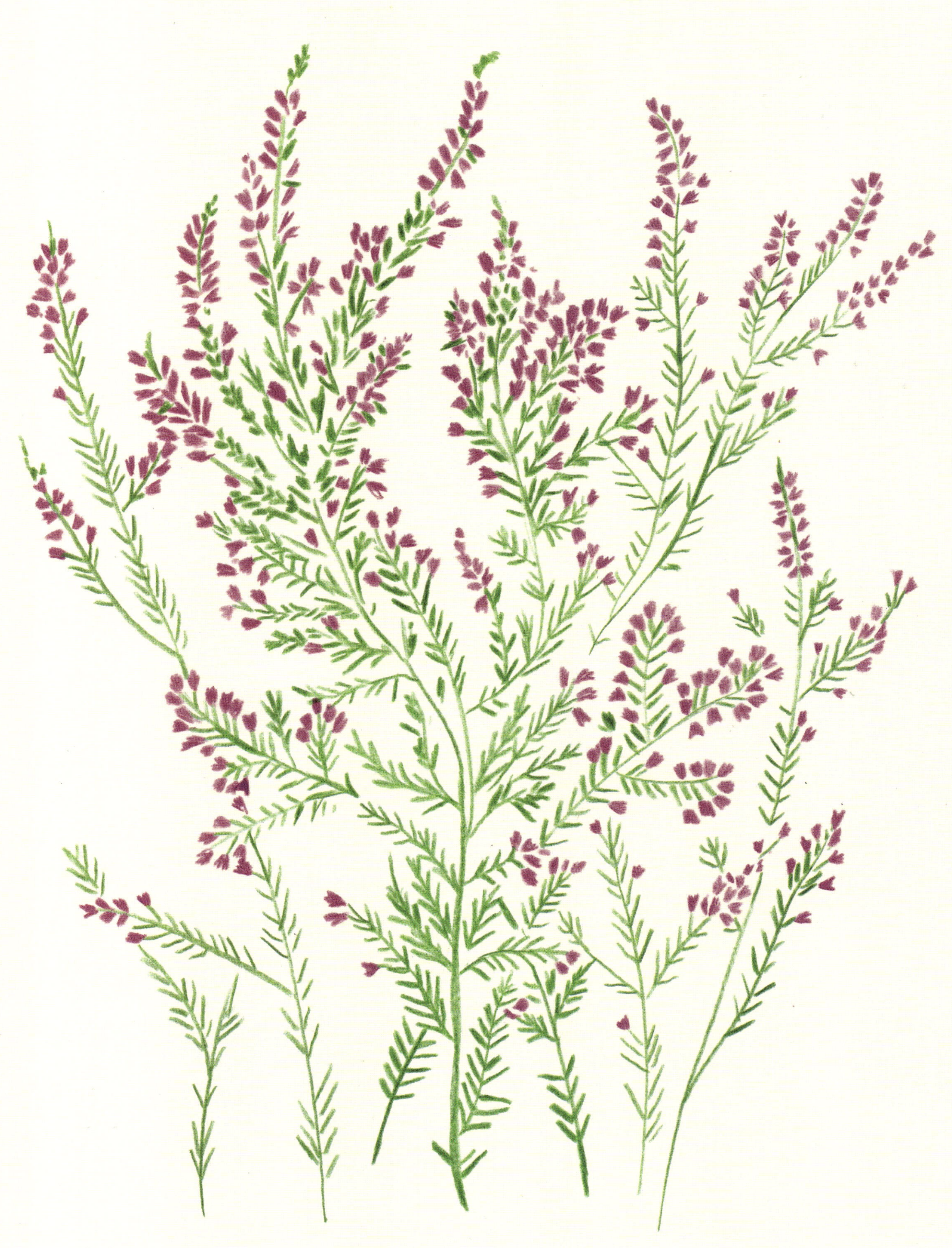

HEATHER

---

**BOTANICAL FAMILY:**
ERICACEAE.

---

**BLOOMS:**
ACCORDING TO THE SPECIES AND VARIETY.

---

**WHEN TO PLANT:**
ALL YEAR LONG.

---

**COLOURS:**
PINK, VIOLET, WHITE.

**H**eather is a shrub that generally flowers in the autumn (*Calluna vulgaris*) or winter (*Erica carnea*), although some species or varieties flower at other times of the year. There are more than 800 known species, of which 90 per cent are native to South Africa. They are differentiated by their flowering time, shape, colour and hardiness, so don't hesitate to ask your local nursery which suits your requirements best. Be that as it may, I love all heathers, and I can only encourage you to adopt them into your gardens.

With its evergreen foliage and tiny, colourful flowers, this cold-resistant plant (generally withstanding temperatures as low as -15°C (5°F)) will add charm to any patch of land. It can be used as an ornamental plant or as groundcover. Considered a melliferous flower (yielding nectar and pollen for honey), its flowering tuffs are often busy with bees.

Heather is often associated with heath- or moorlands, a sign that it adapts well to chalky, poor soils. Growing as it does in desolate or near desert-like landscapes, no wonder that the heather has come to signify solitude in the language of flowers.

It is best situated in full sun but, in more southern climes, semi-shade is preferable. As it decomposes, heather creates a light soil – true ericaceous compost – suitable for planting acid-loving plants. I don't have the space for one in my garden but I would love to have a tree heath, or tree heather – *Erica arborea* can grow as tall as 4m (13ft). True ericaceous magic!

---

ILLUSTRATOR:

# Isabelle Laydier Kristensen

**FRANCE**
@ISABELLELAYDIERKRISTENSEN

**Isabelle lives in France and is the co-founder of** *Blumenhaus*, **a magnificent magazine that celebrates floral art. To capture all the delicacy of heather, Isabelle used coloured pencils – a medium as unpretentious as the flower itself.**

**Carole:** What was your point of departure for your creation?
**Isabelle:** I took my initial inspiration from a lino print, notably for the central branch, then I extended the drawing with branches I saw in a mass of heather near my home.

**Carole:** Did you find this plant hard to depict?
**Isabelle:** Not very – the fact that the clusters of flowers were quite dense gave me a certain freedom.

**Carole:** What do you like about this flower?
**Isabelle:** I like that it blooms for a long time, which gives me the time to appreciate it even more deeply!

*If Isabelle were a flower, she would be* **a Chinese peony.**

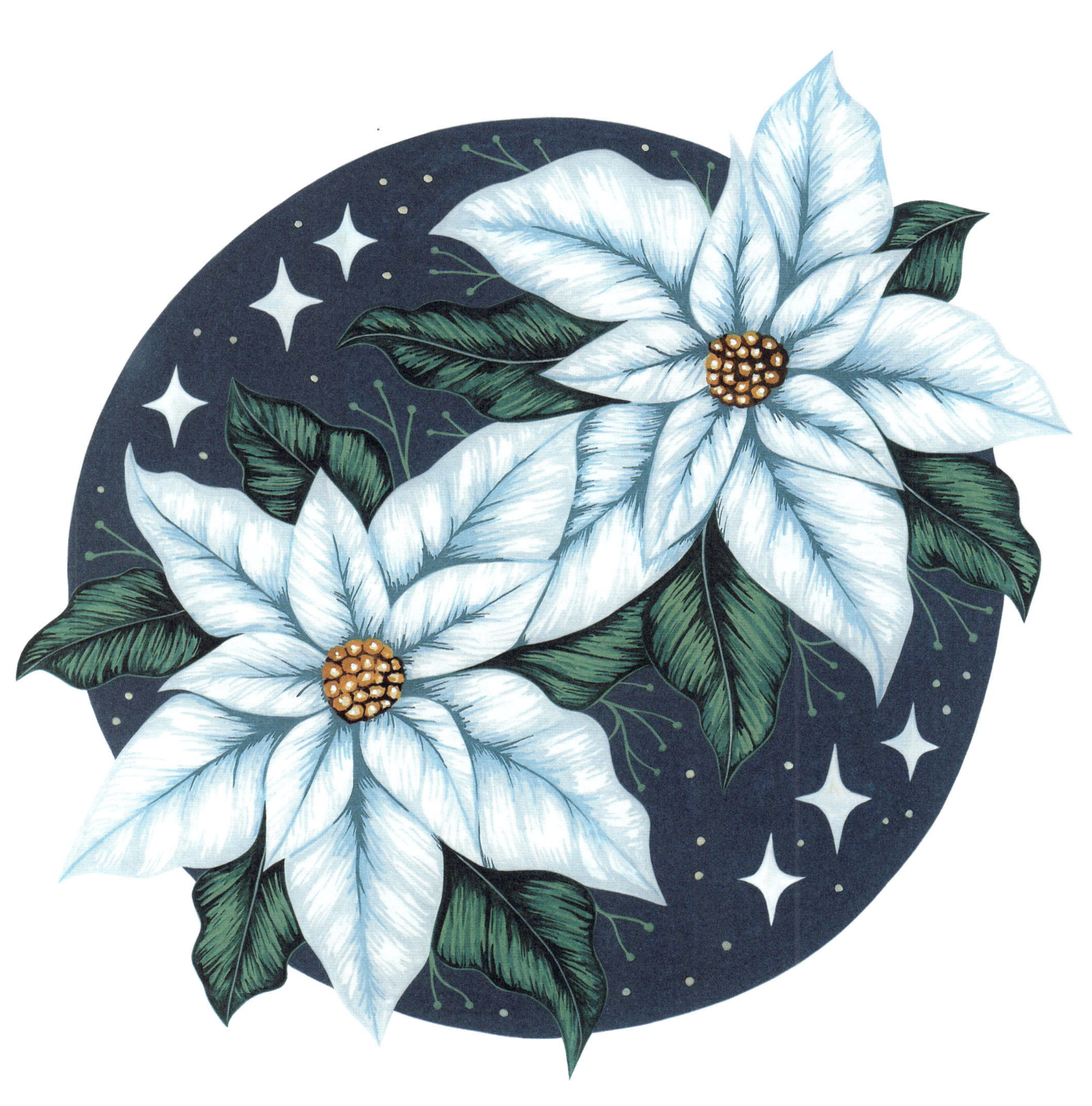

POINSETTIA
OR CHRISTMAS STAR

---

**BOTANICAL
FAMILY:**
EUPHORBIACEAE.

---

**BLOOMS:**
DECEMBER.

---

**WHEN TO PLANT**
JUNE—SEPTEMBER.

---

**COLOURS:**
RED, WHITE, YELLOW,
PINK, CREAM.

# Poinsettia

**T**his plant – sometimes also poetically known as the Christmas star – owes its name to Joel Roberts Poinsett (1779–1851), a botanist and US ambassador to Mexico in the 1820s, who introduced the plant to the United States.

In its natural habit it can grow several metres tall, but we typically think of it as a small compact shrub – often as the small-scale potted indoor version with its circles of deep-red bracts (though I prefer the ones with white bracts as in Becky Amelia's illustration). These, in fact, are not the flowers proper – the actual ones are small and yellow and buried in the midst of the whorl of bracts.

Another peculiarity of these somewhat odd plants is that, in order for them to flower during the end-of-year festivities, they have to follow a strict lighting regime.

From the end of September the shrub is kept in total darkness for 12–14 hours each night: Go on – back into your prison cell, poinsettia! The rest of the time it is placed in indirect sunlight to prevent leaf burn.

It's recommended to water your poinsettia with tepid water once per week during the growing period, and once every ten days when dormant. To maintain, cut the stems after flowering and re-pot every three years …

So, yes, the poinsettia will keep well beyond the holiday period: this is easy enough, and the following year you will be over the moon to see it flower again, heralding the imminent arrival of Father Christmas. I sometimes wonder whether it couldn't even replace the Christmas tree as a way to celebrate the season more ecologically.

---

ILLUSTRATOR:

# Becky Amelia MacCarrick

**UNITED KINGDOM**
@BECKYAMELIA_ART

**This illustration is burned into my retina. The use of both watercolour and gouache reveals all the potential of the poinsettia, as does, of course, Becky Amelia's talent.**

**Carole:** Why are flowers at the heart of your artistic universe?
**Becky Amelia:** Nature's diversity seems unlimited. Shapes, sizes, colours, geometries … this profusion is for me a source of inexhaustible inspiration! From the delicate, tiny-flowered Gypsophila to the showy hydrangea, every flower has a story, and I love to tell these stories through these illustrations.

**Carole:** Where do you go to enrich your work and find inspiration?
**Becky Amelia:** My favourite places in the world are nature parks and botanic gardens such as the Royal Botanic Gardens, Kew, in London. But I also love ecological centres such as the Eden Project and Lost Gardens of Heligan, in Cornwall, where I live.

*If Becky Amelia were a flower, she would be* **a hyacinth**. *She loves to see them pop up here, there and everywhere in the English countryside in spring!*

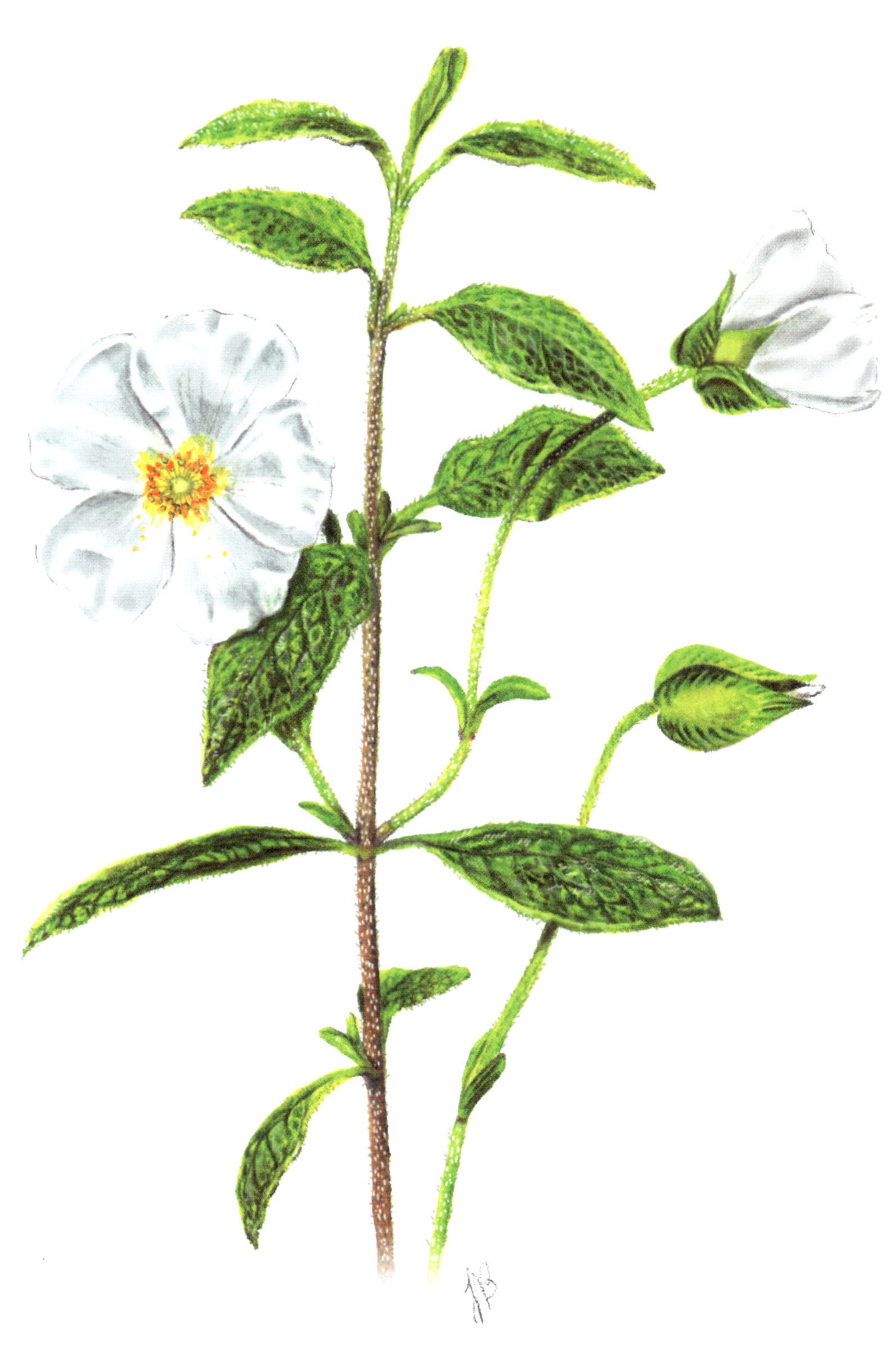

ROCKROSE

**BOTANICAL FAMILY:**
CISTACEAE.

**BLOOMS:**
APRIL–JULY.

**WHEN TO PLANT:**
MARCH–MAY.

**COLOURS:**
WHITE, PINK, PURPLE, YELLOW.

**Flowers least adapted for the garden, like the rockrose (*Cistus* species), have a grace that touches me deeply. On the one hand, in terms of their appearance, they feature five large crumpled petals that look like crêpe paper, and sometimes sport purple-brown patches around their golden centres. On the other hand, they are often short-lived – each rockrose flower lasts just 24 hours. Happily, this perennial shrub flowers repreatedly from April to July, according to the variety. The leaves have a sticky texture and can be anything from deep to silver green. In total, there are around 20 species today, as well as numerous hybrids.**

Rockroses are hardy and can survive droughts, storms and fires. The plant is a pyrophyte – that is, it can regenerate and regrow after a fire. You won't be surprised, then, to discover that it flourishes in dry terrains with poor soils. By contrast, it doesn't do well in the cold – if the temperature falls below -5°C (23°F), things can get complicated!

In the wild the *cistus* is native to the Mediterranean maquis and garrigue scrublands. To capture the spirit of the Côte d'Azur, plant the rockrose in full sun in the company of lavender, rosemary, thyme, sage and Californian poppies.

The rockrose, finally, has an attractive fragrance. The plant is covered with a sticky resin, called labdanum, which protects it and prevents it from drying out. It is also something that has attracted the attention of parfumiers. Whether used as a fixative or as a background note, the rockrose is today used in many perfumes – maybe even yours!

ILLUSTRATOR:

# Julie Borgese

**FRANCE**
@JULIEBOR91

**I met Julie for a media interview and loved chatting with her. Her career as a scientific illustrator fascinates me, and she always replied very carefully to my questions. I love her precision, curiosity and joy in getting all the treasures of nature onto paper.**

Carole: Describe how you went about depicting the rockrose.
Julie: Everything began with a careful study of the plant. Then, using detailed botanical descriptions and photos, I took the time to understand its characteristics because, for me, accuracy is fundamental. Then I went off into nature with my easel and materials (watercolours and fine-grain paper) in quest of my subject.

Carole: In your eyes, is it a difficult flower to depict?
Julie: Yes, especially because of that charming crumpledness! Its petals are very delicate, which gives it a great fragility, and it is this that I've tried to capture.

*If Julie were a flower, she would be **an edelweiss** … She discovered this flower as a child. Because of its zany looks and rarity, the edelweiss has always had a special place in her heart.*

Rockrose

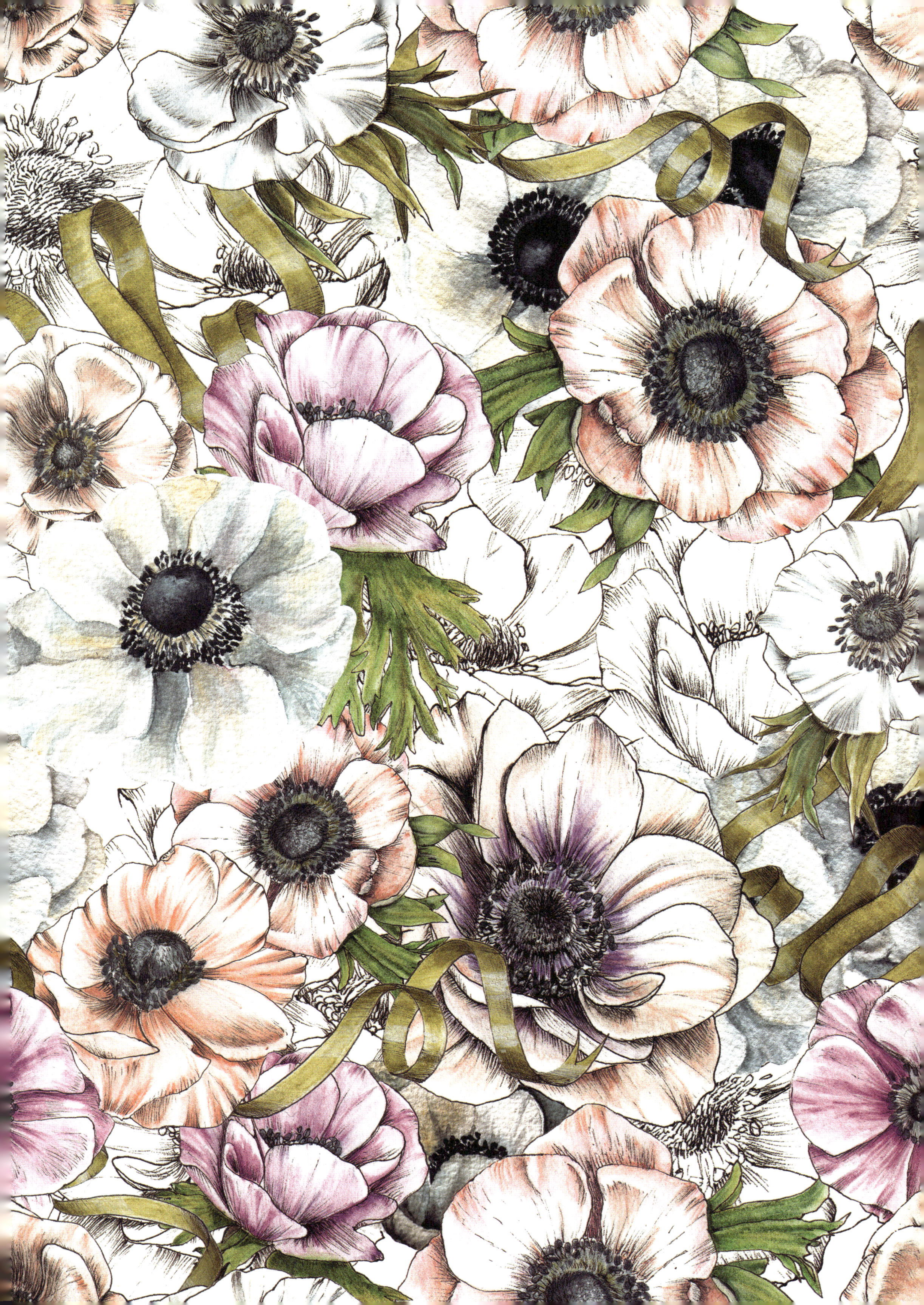

ANEMONE

**BOTANICAL FAMILY:**
RANUNCULACEAE.

**BLOOMS:**
APRIL–MAY AND A POSSIBLE SECOND FLOWERING IN AUTUMN FOR THE POPPY ANEMONE. AUGUST FOR THE JAPANESE ANEMONE.

**WHEN TO PLANT:**
FEBRUARY–APRIL. SEPTEMBER–NOVEMBER.

**COLOURS:**
RED, BLUE, WHITE, PINK, VIOLET.

# Anemone

**A**ppreciated by gardeners for centuries, the anemone is the ubiquitous flower that transcends fashions and times and even has its place in Greek mythology. According to legend, Adonis, the lover of Aphrodite, was fatally wounded by a boar. The drops of his blood, mixed with the tears of the goddess, were said to have brought forth this new plant. It's said that, at each spot where the lovely young man's blood fell, red anemones sprang up. Thus, these flowers came to symbolize lost love and the fragility of life.

My heart seesaws between the crown anemone (*Anemone coronaria*) and the Japanese anemone (*Anemone japonica*).

Among the varieties of the first, I love the classic De Caen anemone 'the Bride'; among the varieties of the second, I have a weakness for 'Regal Swan', with its majestic, dense flower spikes.

If you would like to start a small anemone collection, as I have, you should plant them in well-drained, compost-rich soil, preferably in semi-shade.

These poetic flowers will be a graceful addition to your flowerbeds. You can use the flowers to make pretty bouquets for your dinner table, though perhaps I should use the grander 'banquet table', as anemones often appear in royal and aristocratic gardens.

---

ILLUSTRATOR:

# Alexandra Bodji

**FRANCE**
@ALEXANDRA.BODJI

**I can well imagine that you might be tempted to buy several copies of this book and cut out this illustration multiple times to use like wallpaper. With a black felt-tip pen, watercolour pencils and box of watercolour paints, Alexandra perfectly draws out the contrast between the soft pastel tones of the petaloid sepals and the bluish, even black, heart that accompanies the ring of stamens so characteristic of the anemone.**

Carole: How did you transpose the anemone onto paper?

Alexandra: I took my inspiration from a real bunch of anemones but also from images on Pinterest. It's a flower that wears its heart on its sleeve; it's uninhibited and open to the world; the stamens, too, are very visible.

Carole: Why do flowers inspire you?
Alexandra: I like to depict the elegance and delicacy of flowers. If you take the time to truly look at them, you will be sure to be surprised afresh by their individuality and fragility every time you encounter them.

*If Alexandra were a flower, she would be **a peony**. She adores the spectacle the flowers provide when they open — a vision of luxury and opulence.*

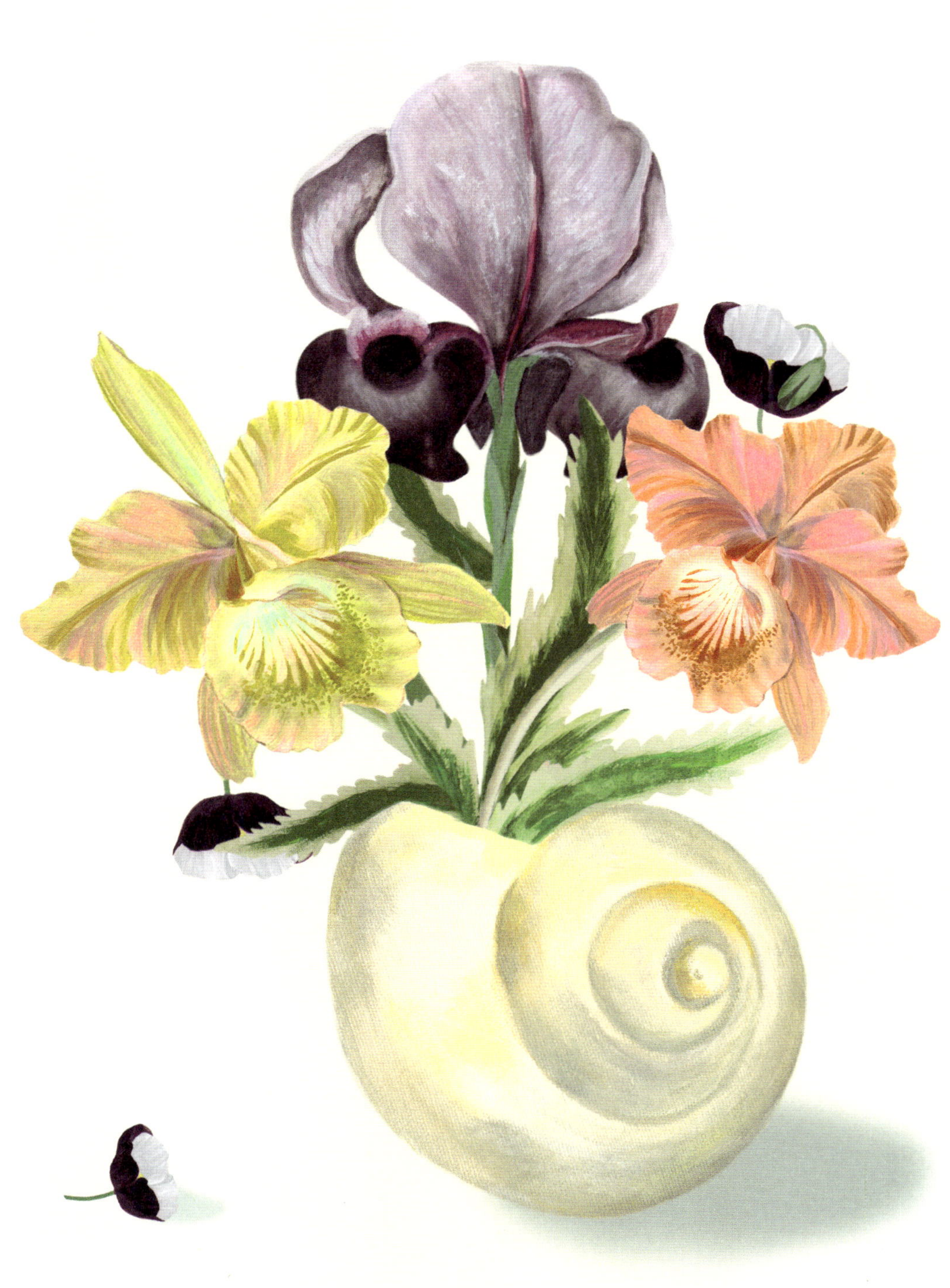

GARDEN IRIS
OR BOG IRIS

**BOTANICAL FAMILY:**
IRIDACEAE.

**BLOOMS:**
MARCH–JUNE
DEPENDING ON
THE SPECIES AND
CLIMATE.

**WHEN TO PLANT:**
IN SUMMER AND
UNTIL OCTOBER IN
MILD CLIMATES.

**COLOURS:**
BLUE, WHITE,
YELLOW, RED, VIOLET,
MULTICOLOURED.


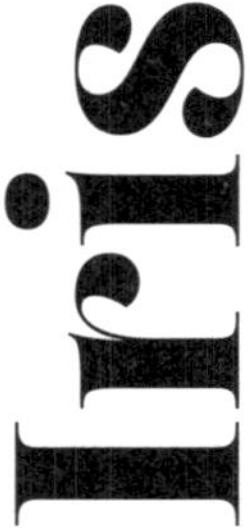

**I**n Greek mythology fleet-footed Iris was the messenger of the gods, the link between the Olympian deities and humankind. I like to think that her floral namesake also acts as a link – between people and their gardens.

This perennial rhizomatous plant is very easy to grow and hence very popular. However, it is important to distinguish between garden and bog (or water) irises. For example, *Iris germanica* adapts well to a hot, dry climate. Bog irises, by contrast, grow well in wetter areas such as the edges of ponds or in marshy ground. In general, however, the iris withstands dry conditions well.

The flowers are famous for their complex beauty. The long narrow leaves show stems 20–120cm (8–47in) in height, according to the variety, topped by butterfly-like flowers made up of three exterior sepals and three interior petals in vivid colours.

If you like the bicoloured look, choose the dependable *Iris germanica* varieties 'Night Edition' and 'Robe du Soir' – which fulfil all the promise of their names. For those who prefer a white iris with a hint of difference, I suggest the *Iris japonica* 'Variegata'.

As a conversational gambit at a dinner party, remember that the iris is the true emblem of the kings of France. While the lily is usually cited as thus today, legend gives the iris this role in the royal coat of arms: according to legend, Clovis (died 511), first king of the Franks, was pursued into marshland by the Visigoths but evaded his pursuers by hiding behind a clump of irises, thereby saving his life and eventually enabling him to be victorious. This flower doesn't have that haughty bearing for nothing.

---

ILLUSTRATOR:

# Mandy Sade

**SWEDEN**
@M_A_N_D_Y_S_A_D_E

**Mandy created this custom-made illustration using gouache on a plywood panel. She has added a element that may surprise when juxtaposed with a garden flower: a seashell. I'll let you tell the story about how a shell and a iris came to meet.**

Carole: How did you 'crack' the iris?
Mandy: I took my inspiration from its organic shapes and its seasonal changes. I always like to add a surrealistic touch to my work, and I am fascinated by interesting and unexpected compositions. I have to say that I found this flower difficult because I've never painted one before. It has an extraordinary structure.

Carole: Where did you get the passion for flowers that shows up in your work?
Mandy: When I was growing up, my parents were always fervent gardeners, and they got a lot of satisfaction out of their colourful country garden. I adored watching the plants grow and learning their strange names.

*If Mandy were a flower, she would be **a peony** to bring happiness to all.*

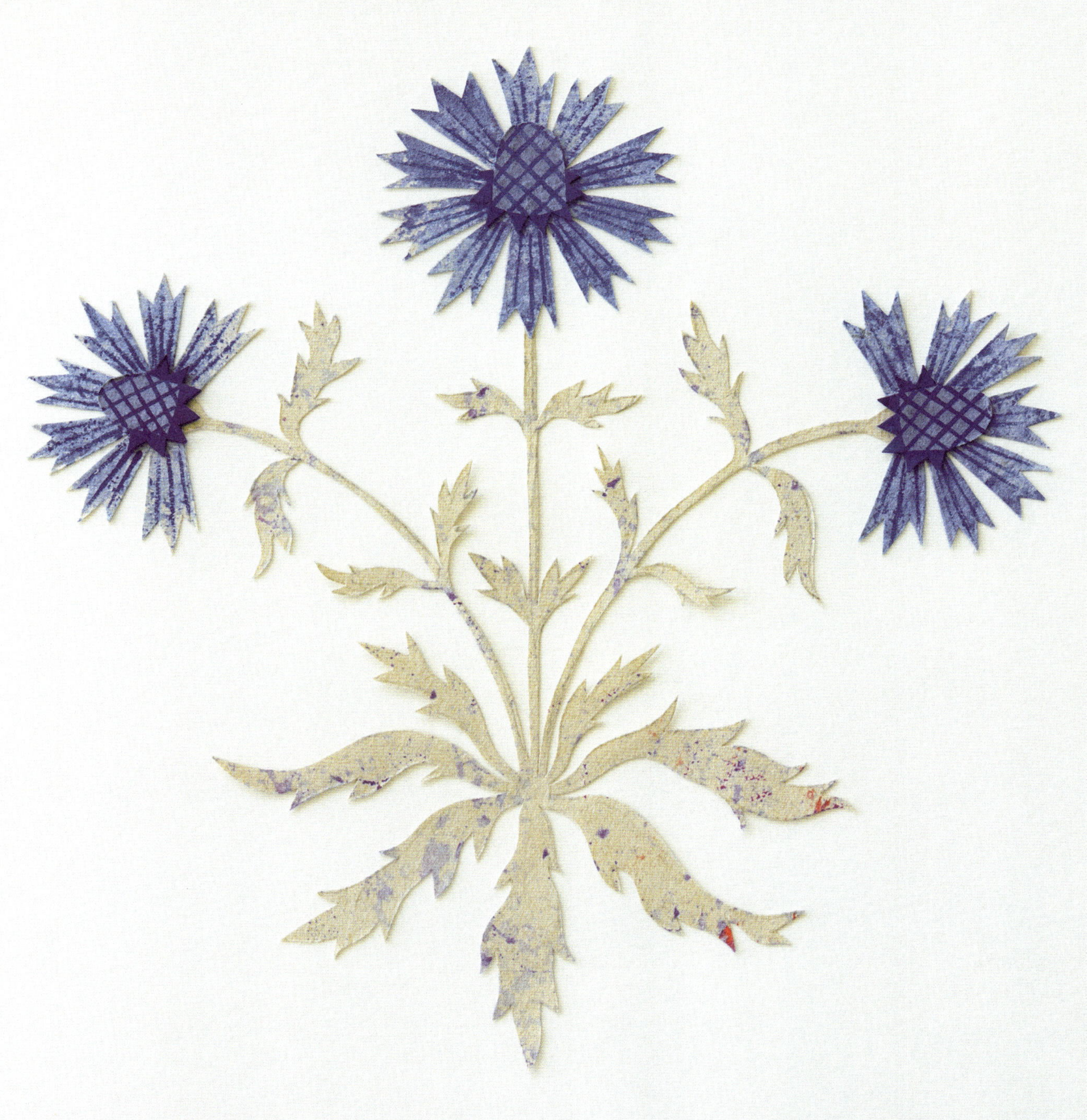

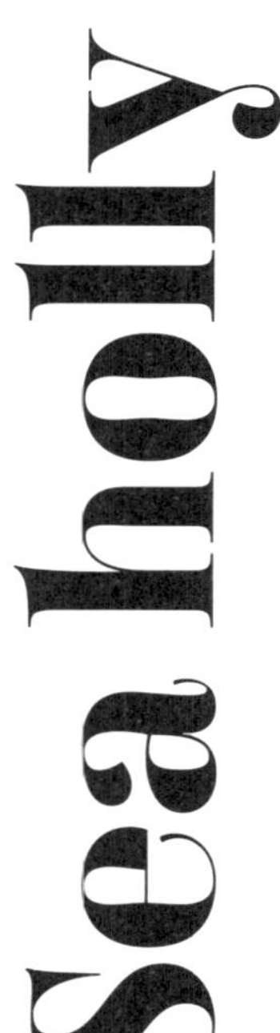

**W**ith its strong stems, green, blue-green or even silver toothed or lobed leaves, and blue, white or green umbels (flower clusters coming from a common point), this herbaceous plant strikes an elegant, graphic pose.

Depending on the species, the sea holly can reach 30–100cm (12–39in) tall, thanks to its robust stem and taproot. The plant puts down deep roots, making it particularly resistant to drought. It doesn't need a lot of watering, but does need sun, to become established. So, choose a spot in full sun when planting. In terms of soil, poor, stony and well-drained will do the trick.

As you will have already gathered, the sea holly is nothing if not robust, so you won't be surprised to learn that it's generally hardy. However, in areas with harsh winters, a mulch around the base of the plant will perhaps be needed to protect it from freezing. The sea holly belongs to the same family as carrots, fennel and celery and, like them, is edible, as well as being used in cosmetics and for its medicinal properties. Since antiquity it has been used a diuretic, to sooth urinary pain and as an anti-inflammatory.

Avoid picking sea holly if you come across it while out walking. It is becoming increasingly rare in the wild, and some sea holly species are protected under law. Buy a specimen, instead, from your garden centre or from an online nursery. Alternatively, buy them as a cut flower, then dry them – you will be able to appreciate their strange piquant beauty at your leisure.

---

ILLUSTRATOR:

# Lucy Panes
**UNITED KINGDOM**
@LUCYPANES

**For this work, the Devon-based illustrator used the sea hollies growing in her garden as her model, especially for the leaves as the plants were not yet in flower. She completed her research on the internet. Lucy worked in gouache and ink, but also used collage.**

Carole: Do you find the sea holly difficult to paint?
Lucy: In fact, it's a flower that's really lovely to depict because it already has such a stylized, architectural shape – so it lends itself to illustration well, I think.

Carole: What is it about flowers that appeals to you visually?
Lucy: I love the sheer number of forms they take, more even than their colours. I live in the midst of the English countryside, so it's not surprising that living things are at the heart of my work.

*If Lucy were a flower, she would be **a geum**, because it begins to display its sun-yellow flowers as early as April, when few other flowers are in bloom, and continues to flower until September.*

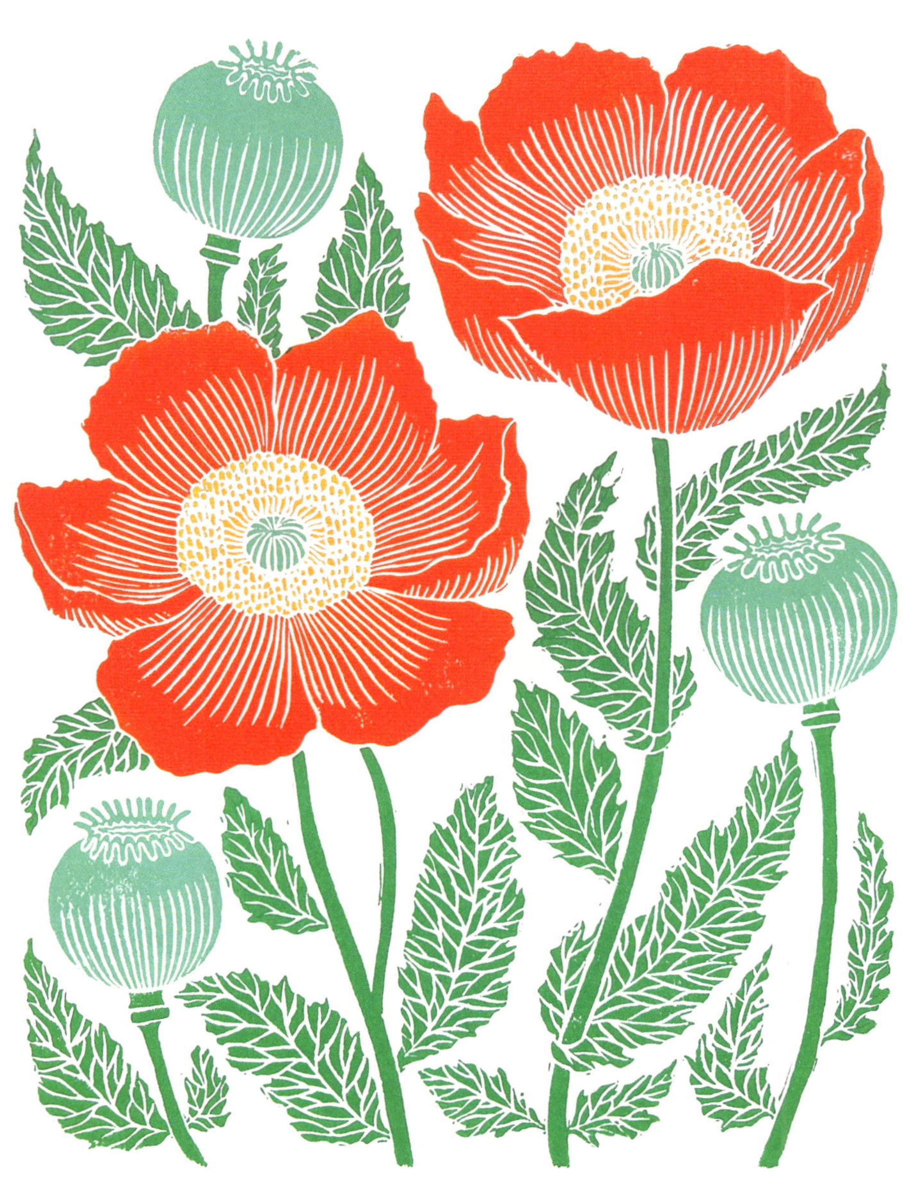

**T**his is the flower that, as children, we love to catch, butterfly-like, in our hands so much are we drawn by its vivid colour and graceful beauty. Poppies, indeed, are as beautiful as childhood itself. I have a very clear memory of gathering poppies by the roadside in my home department, the Ardèche. Today, poppies are no longer so common, due to pesticides, seed sorting and other agricultural techniques, and are no longer a feature of my flower-gathering expeditions. All the same, this iconic segetal flower – one that grows in fields of grain – has not yet breathed its last. Its French name – *coquelicot* – comes from the red of a cockerel's comb. It has become part of history, due to its use in the commemoration of the First World War, as well as part of art history, in the works of Monet, Klimt and Van Gogh.

Found both in town and country, the poppy was for a long time considered a weed but has managed to win us over. Its four, lightly crumpled petals and the fuzzy underside of its leaves lend it a unique beauty. Once cut, the poppy wilts very quickly. To maintain them for longer, burn the ends of the cut stems and be sure to place them in your vase or jug filled only a quarter full of water.

In the garden, the poppy needs a lot of sun but does well in all sorts of soil, with a slight preference for chalky terrains. To sew, rake the soil well and scatter the speeds over a good area. Cover them lightly using your rake. The poppy will self-seed so the next year you have only to watch them regrow and reflower, herald of the return of summer.

ILLUSTRATOR:

# Lili Arnold

**UNITED STATES**
@LILIARNORLDSTUDIOS

**Lili has chosen the block print technique for her rendition of the poppy. I think it modernizes it and plants it more forcefully in the fields of our imagination.**

**Carole:** What, do you think, makes the poppy so individual?
**Lili:** I love the dynamism and delicacy of the way in which the petals are attached to both the stems and the alien-looking seedpods.

**Carole:** What do you appreciate about flowers?

**Lili:** I chose flowers as my preferred subject matter because they owe their beauty to nature and only to nature. I am passionate about the diversity they offer – in height, form and colour. I love watching them sway at the beck and call of the breeze, bathed in sunshine, which often leads me to reflect on their key role in our ecosystem. What's more, flowers seem to bring joy to almost everyone who sees them. They are universally appreciated.

POPPY

*If Lili were a flower, she would be **a Matilija poppy**. She considers the flowers resilient and delicate, combining both strength and beauty.*

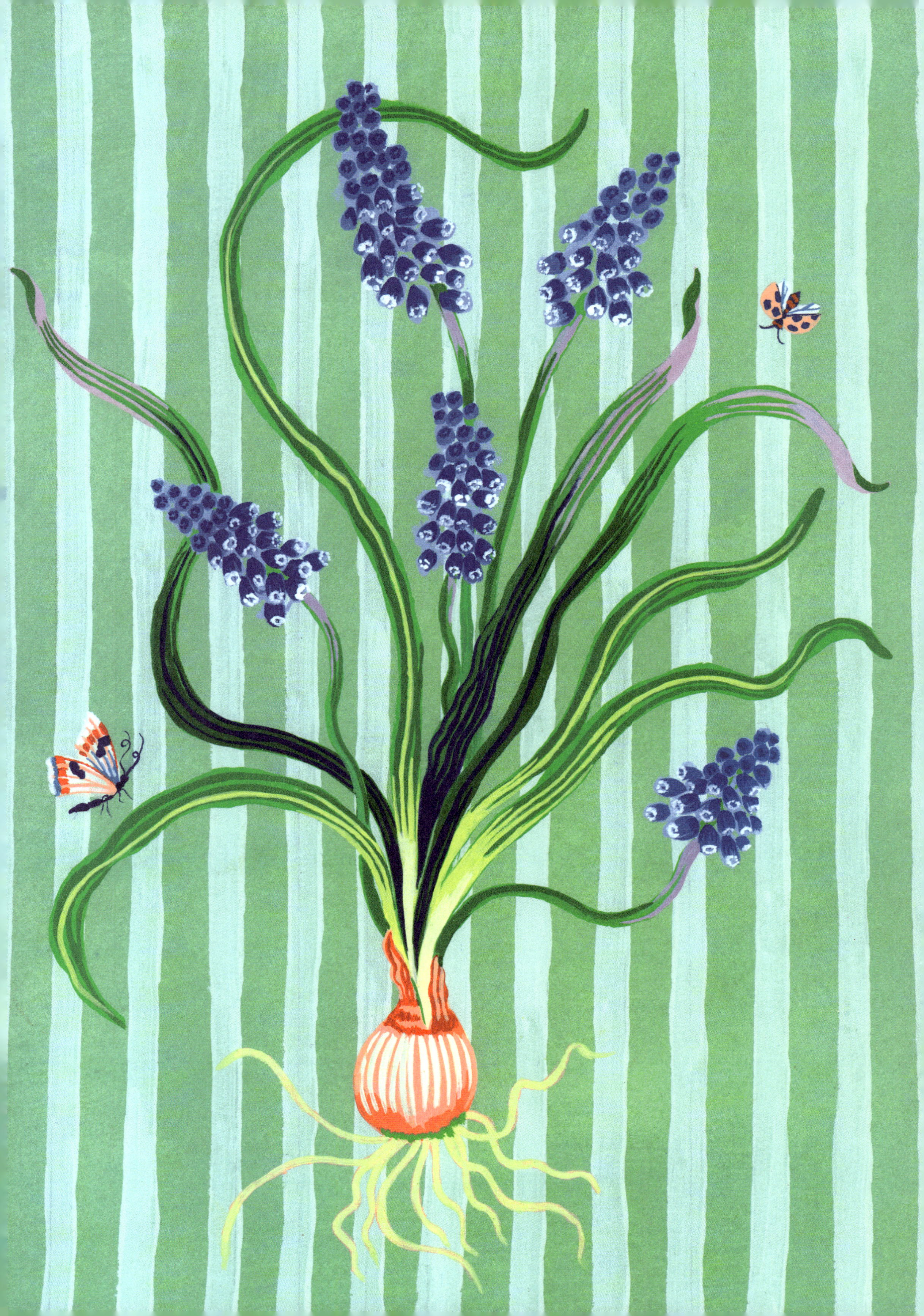

GRAPE HYACINTH
OR MUSCARI

**BOTANICAL FAMILY:**
ASPARAGACEAE.

**BLOOMS:**
MARCH–APRIL.

**WHEN TO PLANT:**
JANUARY–FEBRUARY.
SEPTEMBER–OCTOBER.

**COLOURS:**
BLUE, PINK, WHITE.

# Grape hyacinth

**D**iscreet by nature owing to its height – barely 15cm (6in) tall – the grape hyacinth nonetheless manages to shine because of its beauty. With its tight cluster of vivid blue, intense violet or immaculate white bell-shaped flowers, the grape hyacinth has plenty to offer visually. It is ideal for bringing a touch of colour to a border, rock garden, pot or planter.

Grape hyacinths are supremely easy to plant. Between September and November, get yourself some bulbs and plant them at a depth three times their height, in any type of soil as long as it is well drained and in shade or semi-shade. *A little tip:* ideally, buy your bulbs in September, since this avoids them being kept too long in heated stores. You can keep them in a cool place until you are ready to plant them a little later on.

Once planted, the grape hyacinth will spread (via vegetative and generative reproduction), creating carpets of an unbelievable blue. Make a note of when you planted them in your garden planner, though: you'll need to divide the bulbs every three to four years to encourage regeneration.

If you don't much like the ... let's say 'classic' grape hyacinth, seek out the lesser-known 'Pink Sunrise' variety or the bicoloured 'Mount Hood'.

ILLUSTRATOR:

# Sarah Gordon

**UNITED STATES**
@SARAHGORDONDESIGN

**For this illustration, Sarah used thick cotton-rag paper, acrylics and gouache, and for her background took her inspiration from the stripes that are so fashionable in interior decoration just now. Her muse was a grape hyacinth brought that same day in a local garden centre.**

Carole: Is the grape hyacinth easy to paint?
Sarah: The plant looks complicated but is, in fact, astonishingly easy to paint because of the repetitive roundness of the bell-shaped flowers of each inflorescence. The sole difficulty is to capture the volume and delicacy of the lines on the petals. I love the geometry that each bell-shaped flower brings to the whole of the floral spike, and the deep violet-blue of the petals is one my favourite colours in painting.

Carole: Why do flowers inspire you so much?
Sarah: I've always had an emotional bond with nature, which gives me both serenity and positivity. I particularly like flowers and am deeply moved by their unique characters.

*If Sarah were a flower, she would be **a wildflower** blooming joyously in a meadow in a gentle breeze.*

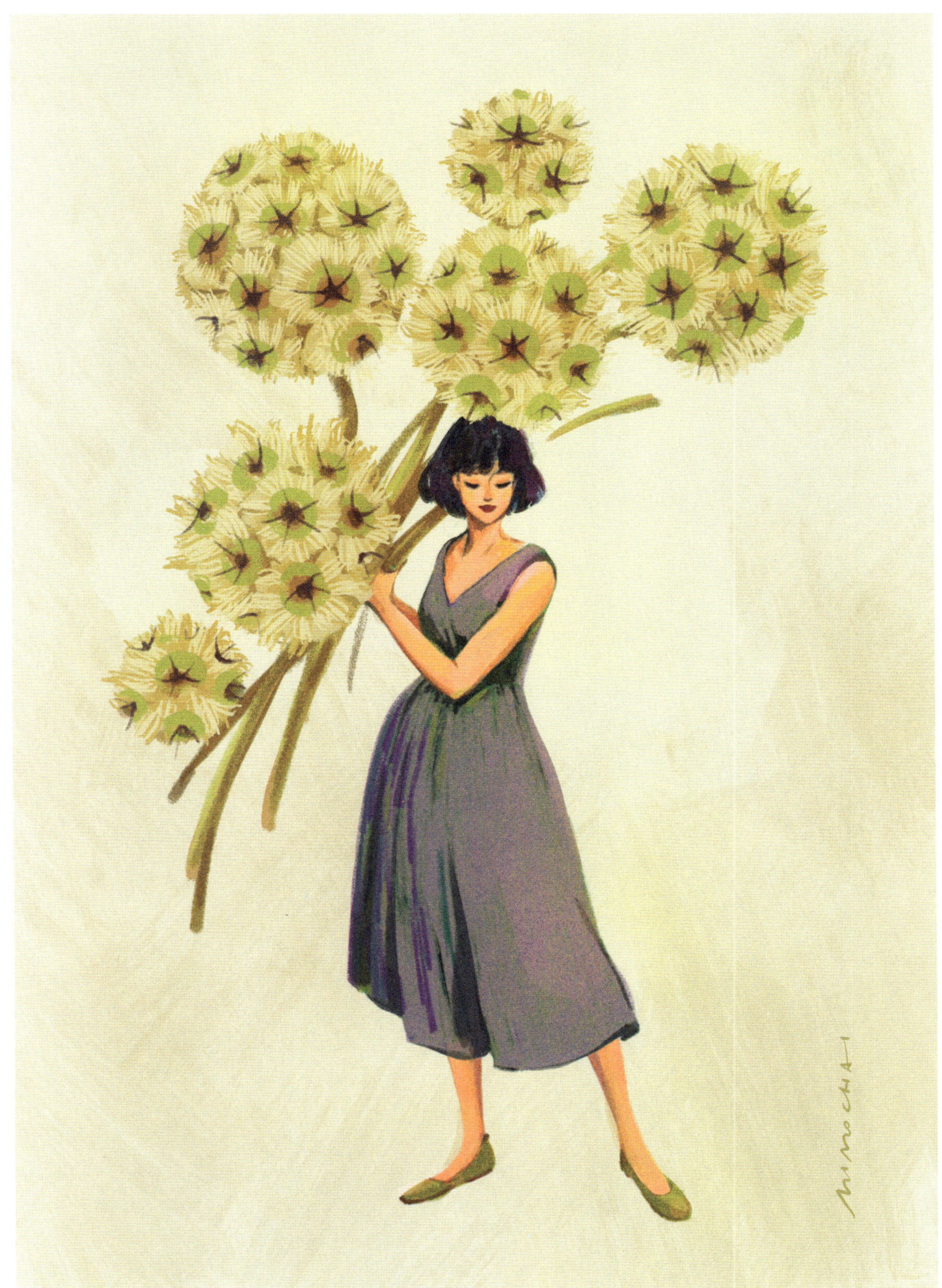

SCABIOUS

**BOTANICAL FAMILY:**
CAPRIFOLIACEAE.

**BLOOMS:**
MAY–JUNE FOR PERENNIALS; JUNE–AUGUST FOR ANNUALS.

**WHEN TO PLANT:**
SPRING AND AUTUMN.

**COLOURS:**
VIOLET, WHITE, PURPLE, YELLOW, BLUE, RED.

# Scabious

**I**f you want to bring a rustic feel to your garden or are a lover of dried flowers, then scabious is the plant for you. There are around 60 species, all of which are sure to satisfy both these needs – these wildflowers of the fields love to grow among tall grasses, and drying them shows off their graphic qualities as well as their durability.

The star among the scabious that are perfect for drying is the *Scabiosa stellata* whose clusters of globular flowers seem to come from another planet. Another surprising species is *Scabiosa ochroleuca* with its unusual pale-yellow flowers.

Here's a quick planting guide:
• Propagate seedlings under cover in March for April planting after the last frosts. Sow the seeds around 1cm (½in) deep and water regularly.
• Plant your scabious in a light, fertile, well-drained soil that can be either slightly alkaline or neutral, and in full sun.
• Alternatively, scatter seeds in a well-loosened soil, enriched with humus and coarse (horticultural) sand.

The scabious – a herbaceous plant that can be either perennial or annual – will impress with its copious blooms. Since it is melliferous, it attracts pollinators, so is a good addition to a spot close to your vegetable patch. It is just as good for pollinating other plants in your garden. All in all, it is a flower whose multiple attractions make it an ideal lifelong companion for the gardener.

---

ILLUSTRATOR:

# Mimi Chao

**UNITED STATES**
@MIMIZCHAO

**The woman depicted in this illustration originally featured in another of Mimi Chao's works, and she straightaway caught my eye. As she originally held flowers other than the scabious, I asked Mimi whether she would agree to change her bouquet. Photographs, imagination, coloured pencils, gouache and digital manipulation all played their part, and scabious: Mimi's version was born!**

**Carole:** What do you like about this flower?

Mimi: One day, I was in a pretty boutique and the owner offered me, just like that, for no reason, a little bunch of dried scabious. This little gesture made my day, and I found the flowers so unique, so enchanting. When you asked me to draw some scabious flowers, I saw it as a little wink from the Universe.

**Carole:** Why do flowers inspire you so much?
**Mimi:** They symbolize human life so well. A slow maturing that is brief, cyclical and universal.

*If Mimi were a flower, she would be **a Californian poppy** for its wild, luminous beauty. What's more, it is a species native to her home state.*

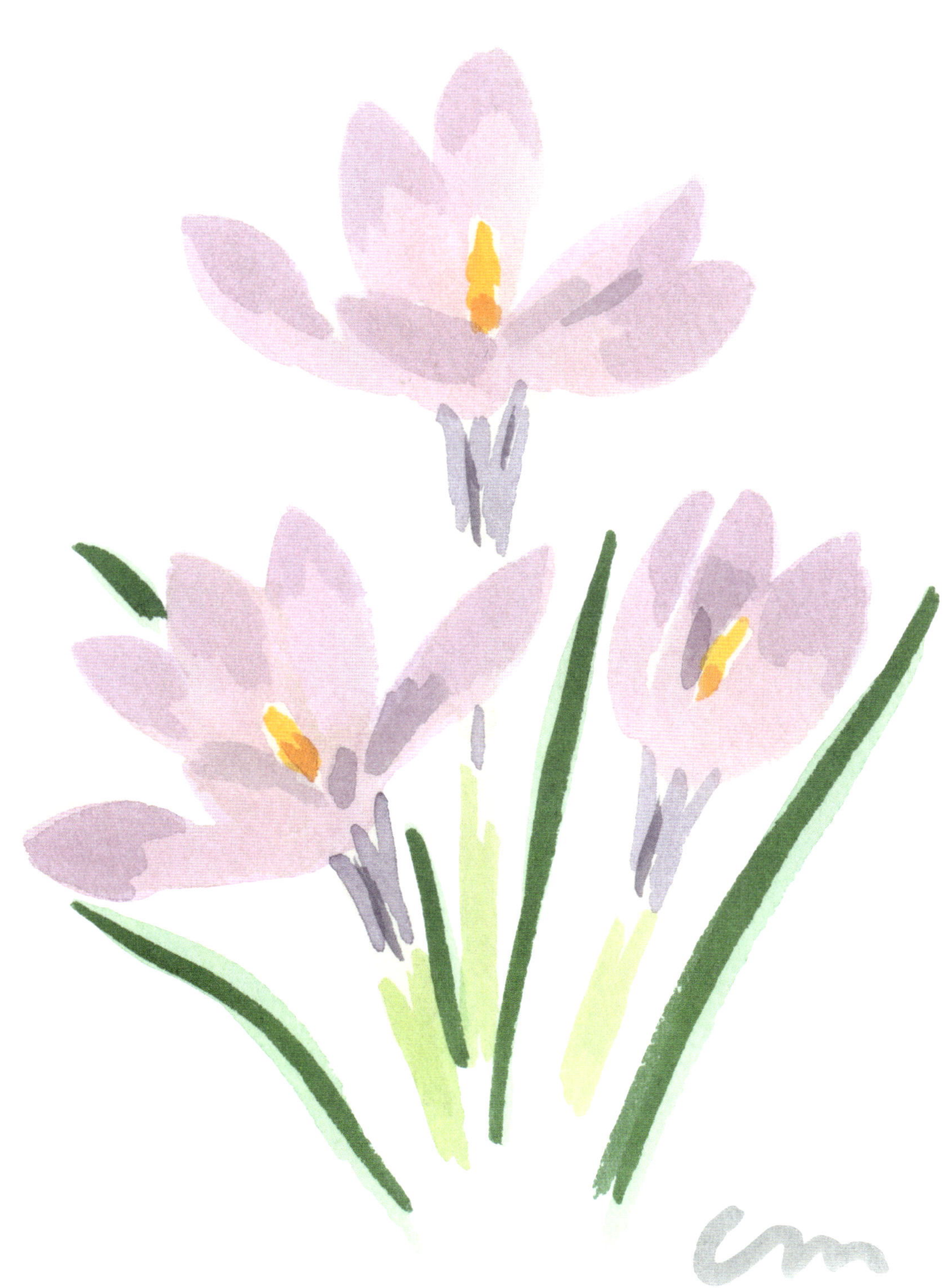

**BOTANICAL FAMILY:**
IRIDACEAE.

**BLOOMS:**
FEBRUARY–APRIL
(SPRING CROCUSES);
SEPTEMBER–
NOVEMBER (AUTUMN
CROCUSES).

**WHEN TO PLANT:**
AUGUST–OCTOBER.

**COLOURS:**
WHITE, BLUE, VIOLET,
YELLOW.

The crocus is a deeply endearing flower for several reasons. First of all, because of its name, which is easy to remember and amusingly prosaic. Then, because of how these tiny intrepid flowers herald spring even as we are still in the grip of winter. Finally, the crocus can make you rich – not any old crocus, of course, but the famous *Crocus sativus,* the saffron crocus with its violet-blue petals and three red stigmas that was perhaps originally grown in ancient Mesopotamia – 'red gold' that currently (summer 2025) sells for around £2,400–£3,200 per kilogram. Enough to make you want to set yourself up as a saffron grower!

There are around 80 species of crocus in total, divided into two main types: spring-flowering and autumn-flowering. If you want an early exit from winter – at least visually – you should plant *Crocus chrysanthus* 'Cream Beauty' with its delightful precocious buds of creamy yellow, or the refined 'Lady Killer', which has violet-and-white flowers. I also love the star-like *Crocus fleischeri* with its elegantly slender petals. For a spectacular early-spring display, you can do little better than a whole carpet of colourful crocuses. Whether single-coloured or bicoloured, crocuses offer an array of colour combinations.

Crocuses like a friable, sandy soil and a spot in sun or semi-shade. Once they have finished flowering, allow the foliage to dry out before cutting back. No need to dig the bulbs out: they will easily multiply from one year to the next. In short, the crocus needs little attention.

---

ILLUSTRATOR:
# Caitlin McGauley
**UNITED STATES**
@CAITLINMCGAULEY

**Based in a gorgeous house next to Lake Mohawk in New Jersey, Caitlin creates textiles and wallpaper print designs for prestigious companies.**

**Carole:** When we contacted you about this book, crocuses weren't in flower, so how did you go about this project?

**Caitlin:** Ideally, I like to paint after nature, but when that's not possible I rely on the photos I take all year long. I have around 2,000 flower photos saved on my phone. I'm really happy to have painted this crocus; it's the first flower I see in my garden each spring, sometimes when the ground is still covered in snow. It is a very hopeful sign.

**Carole:** Is it tricky to paint the crocus?

**Caitlin:** I think that, if I adopted a photorealistic approach, every flower would be extremely difficult to reproduce. Happily, I'm looking for something other than realism so my work is much freer. I paint in layers: I begin the petals with soft, gentle colours and then build up darker shades on top. The challenge is to give the impression of effortlessness.

*If Caitlin were a flower, elle she would be **a daffodil**. She aspires to be as joyful as this flower!*

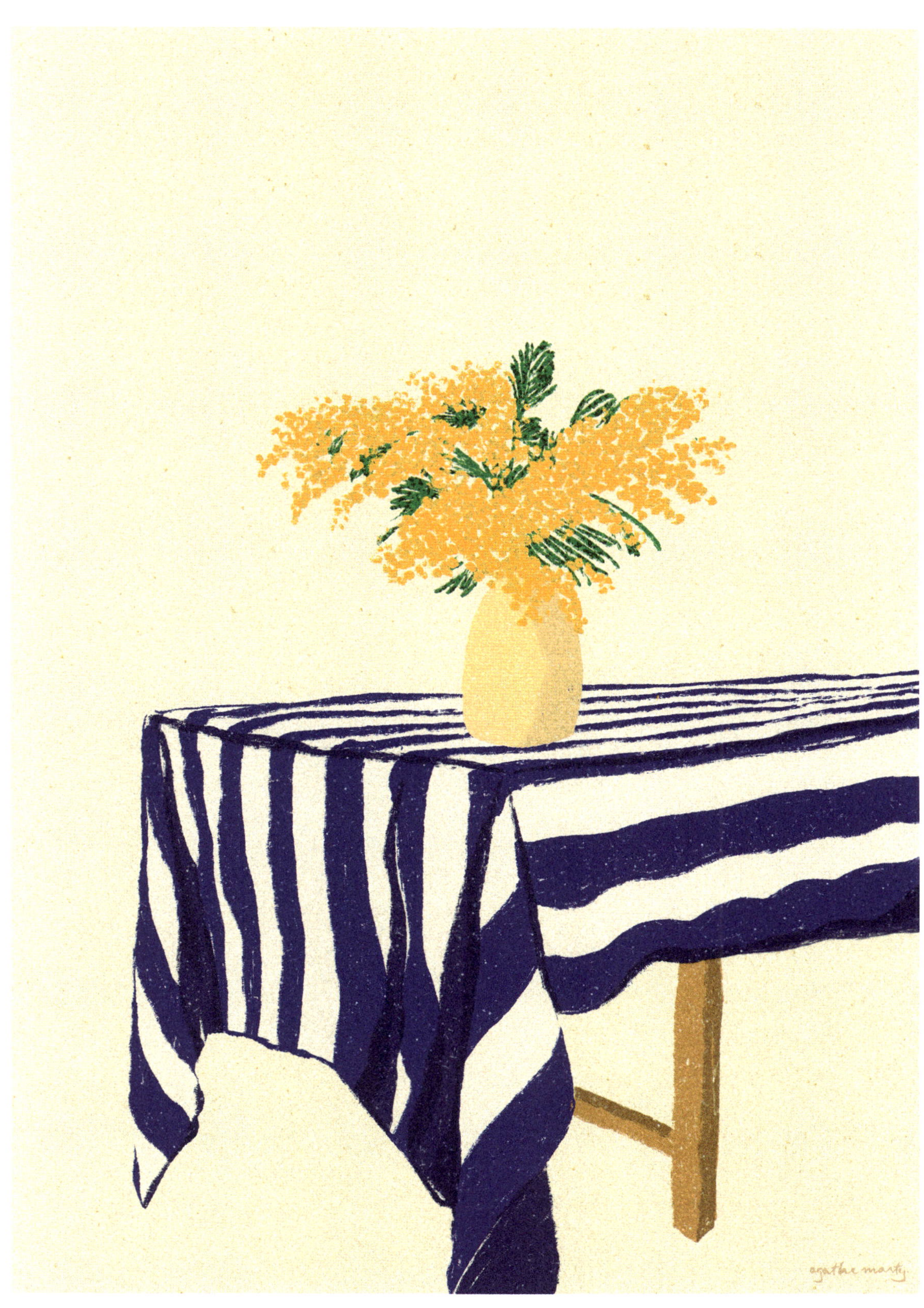

MIMOSA

---

**BOTANICAL FAMILY:**
FABACEAE.

---

**BLOOMS:**
JANUARY–MARCH.

---

**WHEN TO PLANT:**
MARCH–JUNE.

---

**COLOURS:**
YELLOW.

# Mimosa

**A**lthough it originally came from Australia, the mimosa tree has nonetheless become a symbol of my native region – the Côte d'Azur. I have a deep personal attachment to the shrub because I was married in a town named after it – Bormes-les-Mimosas – which took on its sobriquet in 1968 as so many mimosa trees grow there. I love to see its dazzling yellow in my parents' garden from mid-winter on, or hung over festival floats like vegetal sunshine.

This tree, which belongs to the acacia family, needs a warm, frost-free climate and a spot in full sun. It prefers well-drained, sandy, acidic-to-neutral soils (pH6–7). It doesn't tolerate heavy, clayey soils that retain too much water.

While the clusters of its dense vivid yellow blossom are impressive, the mimosa tree has its darker side, too: the mimosa variety *Acacia dealbata* is invasive. It grows very quickly and stifles neighbouring natives. It can also alter the composition of the soil, thereby affecting the micro-habitats of local plants and animals – though it is only the *Acacia dealbata* that is considered 'an invasive alien species'. In the garden, you can, in confidence, choose one of the 1,200 varieties of the plant on offer.

Finally, we should pay homage to one of the mimosa tree's most distinctive qualities: the magnificent, feathery green or bluish foliage.

---

ILLUSTRATOR:

# Agathe Marty

**FRANCE**
@AGATHEM.ILLUSTRATION

**Agathe lives very close to mimosa trees in the South of France. This daughter of the sun loves to work digitally. A tablet and a stylus are all she needs to summon forth some lovely harmonies.**

**Carole:** Do you think the mimosa is difficult to paint?
**Agathe:** Yes, I do. To give the impression of an abundance of those little pompons, you have to draw them one by one. So it's a very painstaking job.

**Carole:** What inspires you creatively when you see mimosa?
**Agathe:** Mimosa provides one of the first blossoms of the year, a sign that spring has at last arrived. The inflorescences are self-contained enough to immediately evoke the idea of spring sunshine by themselves. That's why I decided to paint just the flowers on the table. The natural beauty of the mimosa and the vibrant colour of its little pompoms are very inspirational for me. In this illustration I wanted to transcribe their beauty and share the wonder I feel in front of the first mimosas in flower.

*If Agathe were a flower, she would be **a lotus**. She considers it magnificent and, what's more, it comes from Asia, her favourite holiday destination.*

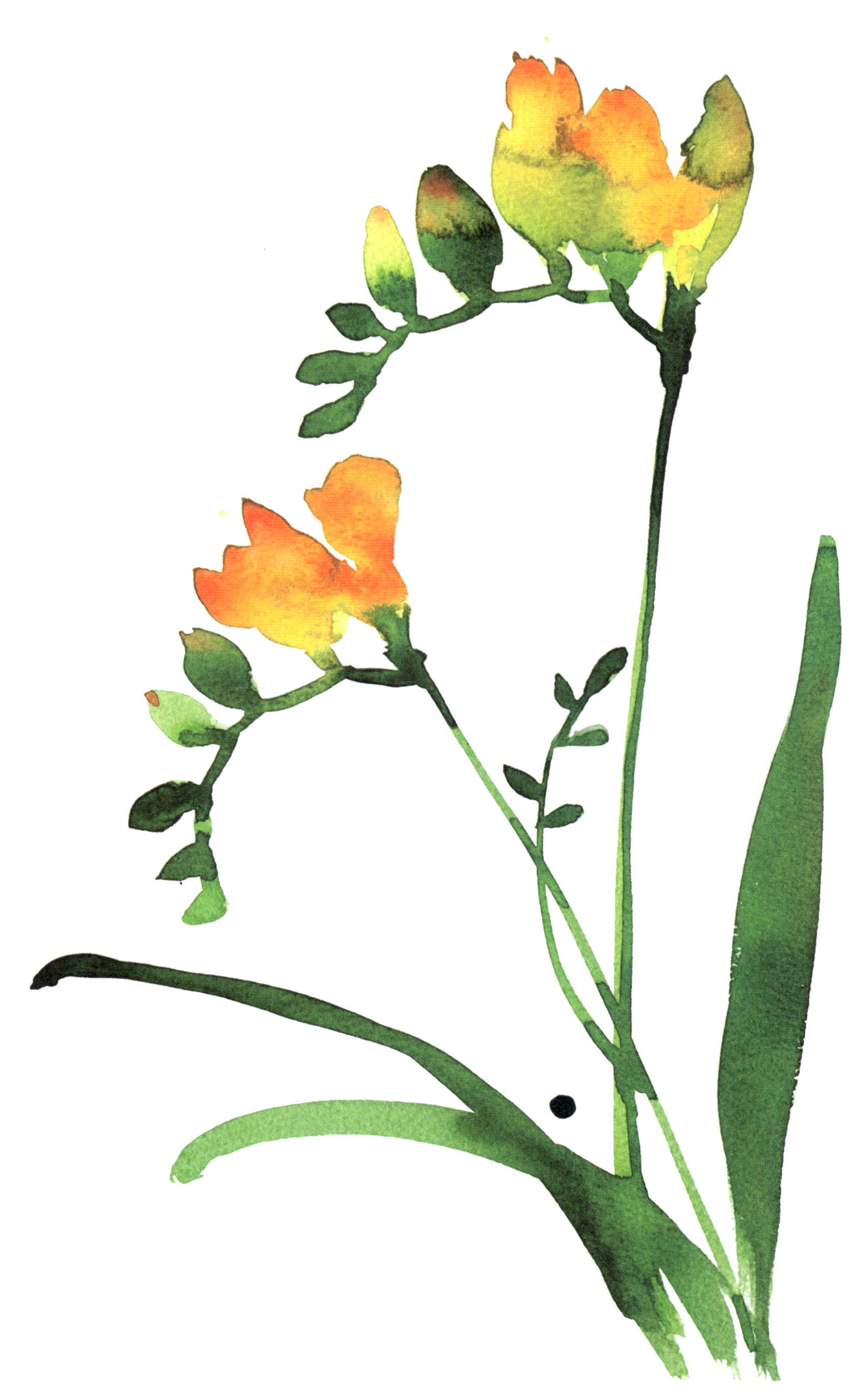

Freesia

FREESIA

**BOTANICAL FAMILY:**
IRIDACEAE.

**BLOOMS:**
MAY–AUGUST.

**WHEN TO PLANT:**
IN SPRING AFTER
THE LAST FROSTS;
IN AUTUMN IF THE
CLIMATE IS MILD.

**COLOURS:**
WHITE, BLUE, PINK,
YELLOW, RED.

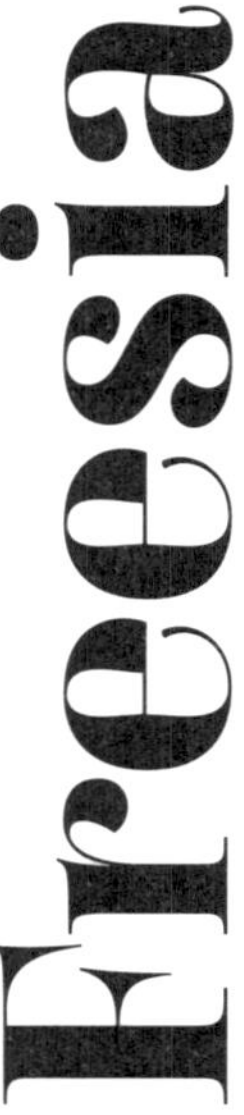

**T**he freesia is another natural wonder. This ornamental bulbous plant (corm) with its narrow, ribbon-like, seasonally shed leaves has a floral spike that grabs all the attention. In a supple curve that turns almost 90 degrees, the plant displays a cluster of flowers arranged along the top side of its upper stem.

This fine yet robust plant can be used to create a bouquet in the ikebana style. This Japanese floral art emphasizes the beauty of the flower according to precise harmonies and time-honoured principles. But those who love pared-back bouquets can replicate  the effect by arranging freesia using an ikebana *kenzan* (spiked flower holder). I find this very beautiful, uncluttered and chic.

In the garden, freesias like full sun and well-drained, lightly acidic soils. It's possible to grow them in pots, even, perhaps, as part of a 'bulb lasagna', in which several types of bulbs are layered up in the same container. This is an excellent way to enjoy the sweet smell of the freesia so prized in perfumery!

A short guide to lasagna planting:
• With their pointy tips uppermost, plant the freesia bulbs around 5–7cm (2–2½in) deep and spaced 10cm (4in) apart.
• Add other bulbs either above or below.
This will allow you to play with various heights of flowers, and to create a spring display generously brimming with blooms.

ILLUSTRATOR:

# Yuliya Podlinnova

**RUSSIA**
@WHITEHEARTDESIGN

**Yuliya lives and works in a small town in the Ural Mountains. She tells me that painting has helped her to see the unique beauty of every flower. Before she embarked on her career as an artist, there were flowers she liked and others she didn't. Drawing them helped change the way she looked at them.**

Carole: How did you manage to give your freesia such a strong presence?
Yuliya: I paint in watercolours, using both the wet-on-wet and west-on-dry techniques (that is, working on damp paper or not). Here I began working wet-on-dry for the flowers and leaves and then added shade using wet-on-wet. Where I live in the Urals we have long winters and brief summers, so it's not always easy to find fresh flowers. To help me I look at photos.

Carole: Would you say it's hard to paint flowers?
Yuliya: Unlike with painting people or animals, getting the proportions right is not so important with flowers. This is an advantage with watercolour as the outcome is unpredictable. I don't always know what the result will be or how the paint will flow across the page.

*If Yuliya were a flower, she would be **a tulip** for its petals that are at once sturdy and delicate – qualities that she finds quintessentially feminine.*

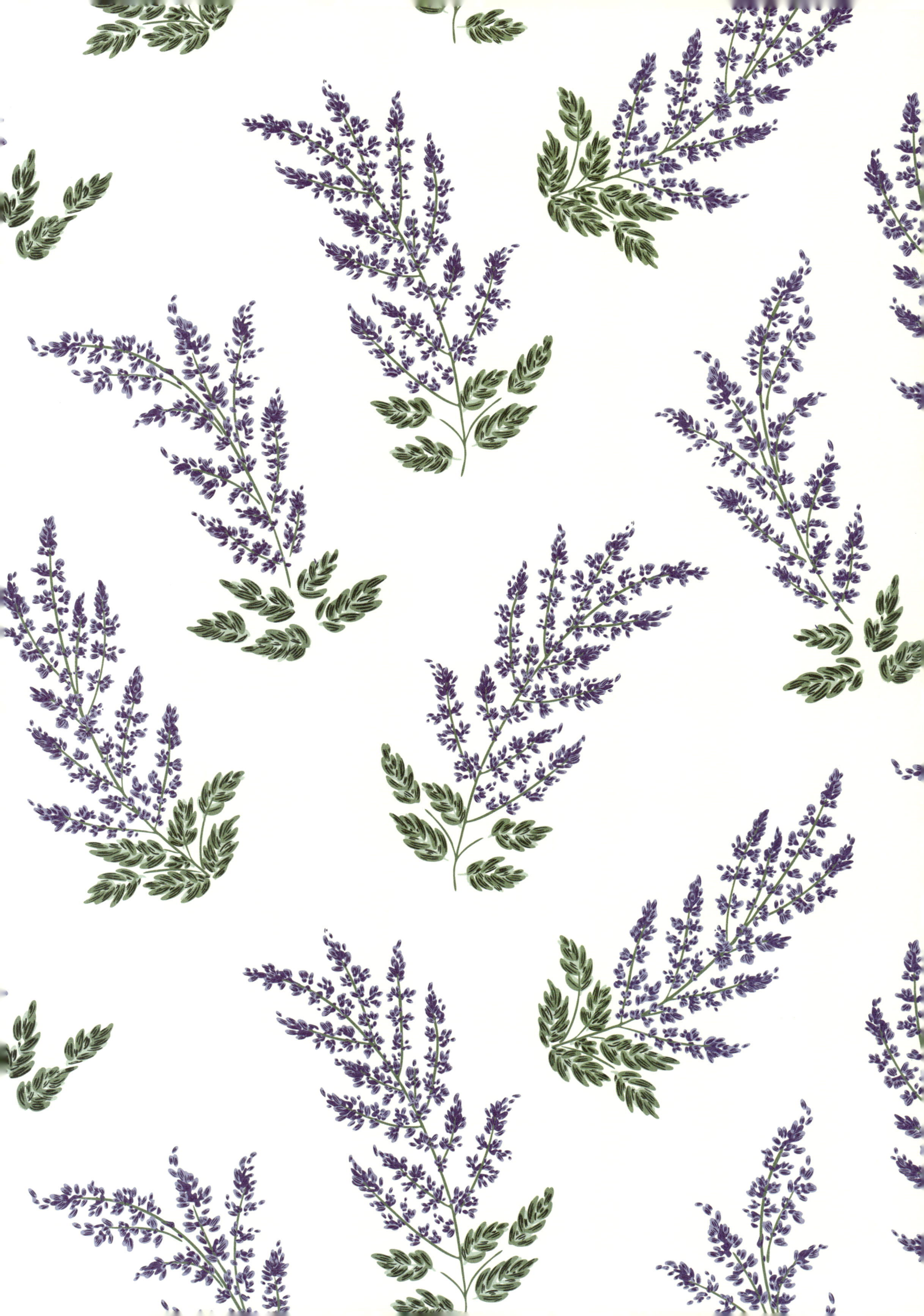

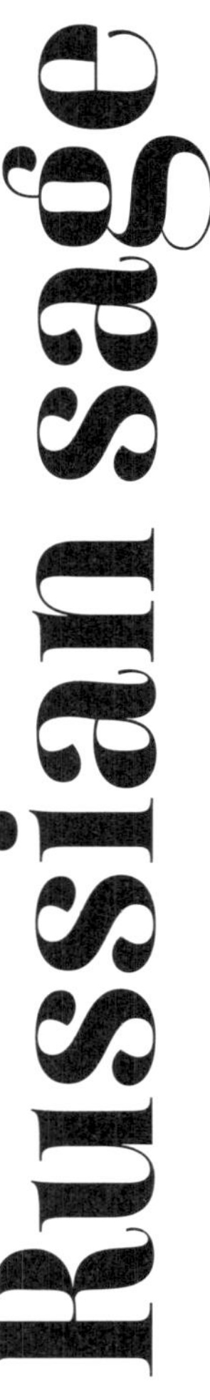



RUSSIAN SAGE

**BOTANICAL
FAMILY:**
LAMIACEAE.

**BLOOMS:**
JULY–SEPTEMBER.

**WHEN TO PLANT:**
MARCH–MAY.
SEPTEMBER–
NOVEMBER.

**COLOUR:**
VIOLET.

**I**magine Russian sage growing in an old stone-built hamlet bathed in sunshine. Welcome to one of my summer hideaways in the Ardèche. I love this plant especially for its silvery foliage and the dazzling mauve of its flowers which harmonizes so well with the blinding summer sunlight. I love to watch it sway in the breeze opposite the front door of my family home. Despite its name, it has its origins in Tibet and other Asian countries.

It is easy to mistake Russian sage for lavender, but it flowers for longer and does not have the same fragrance. It is a joy to see it blooming all summer long, managing to look, I think, both wild and refined at the same time.

It likes full sun and well-drained, even dry, soil. It can grow as high as 120cm (4ft) and 80cm (2½ft) wide, and can be easily propagated by taking cuttings.

For a less imposing variety, you might try *Perovskia atriplicifolia* 'Lacey Blue', which at maturity measures 50cm (20in) in all directions. It's perfect for sunny balconies and terraces, especially next to the sea.

Russian sage is bound to become better known – our warming climate and dwindling natural resources mean that this small shrub, which requires no watering, is cold resistant and attracts pollinators, will doubtlessly make itself ever more useful in our gardens.

ILLUSTRATOR:

# Kashmira Jayaprakash
**INDIA**
@KAYSILLUSTRATIONS

**Kashmira makes and sells her art in the Indian state of Kerala. She is a prolific textile print designer, so you may well already have one of creations close at hand – on a mobile phone cover, a pair of trousers, a pencil case … Her floral prints are everywhere, even on your sitting-room wall if you frame this print!**

Carole: What technique did you use for this work?
Kashmira: I use, in fact, a combination of both hand and digital drawing. I made some ink sketches, then, using the Procreate app, I added coloured washes and the finer details. Then I vectorized the image elements and composed a final layout in Adobe Illustrator.

Carole: How do flowers effect you?
Kashmira: Flowers make me feel happy in an instant. Their colours, shapes and textures fascinate me. Infinitely diverse, every flower has its own unique characteristics. They add such beauty to the world that I can never tire of them.

*If Kashmira were a flower, she would be **a lotus**.
She loves its combination of femininity and strength.*

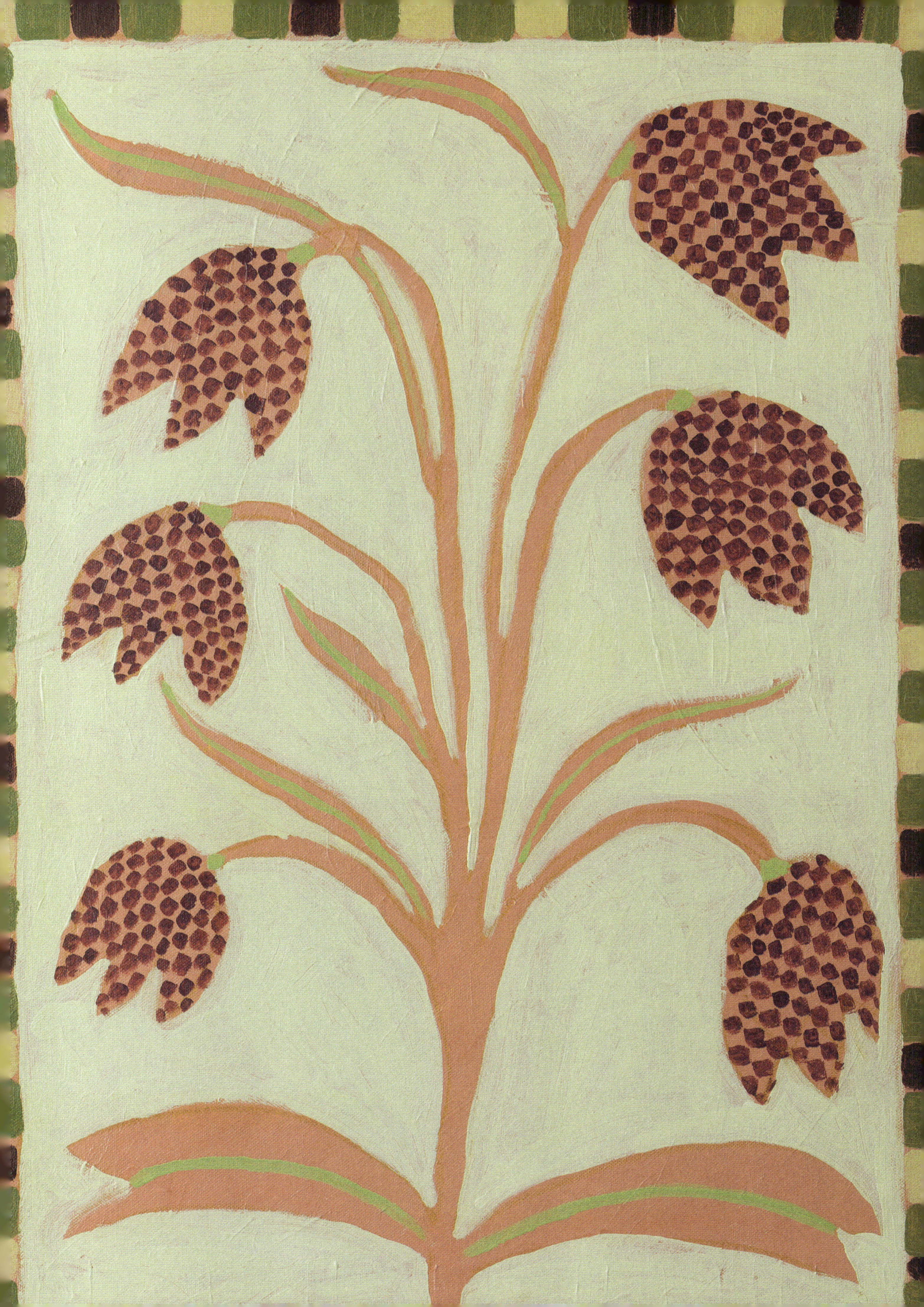

FRITILLARY
OR SNAKE'S HEAD

**BOTANICAL
FAMILY:**
LILIACEAE.

**BLOOMS:**
MARCH–APRIL.

**WHEN TO PLANT:**
OCTOBER–NOVEMBER.

**COLOURS:**
MULTICOLOURED,
PURPLE, PINK
AND WHITE.

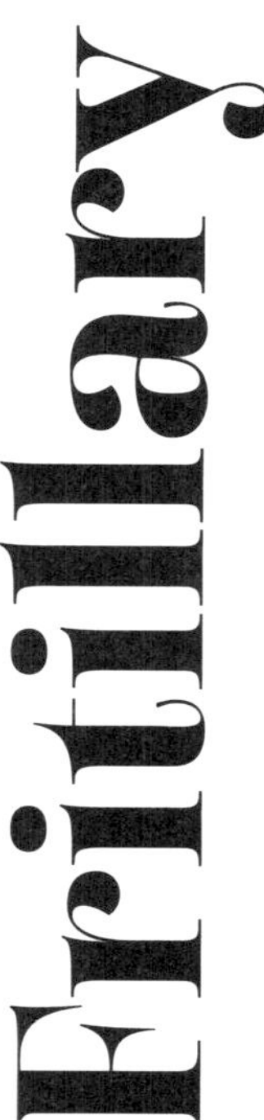

**T**he fritillary (*Fritillaria meleagris*) **is a painting on a stem – we need no other proof that nature is a designer! Both wild and graceful, it gets its species epithet because it is dappled like a guinea fowl (*meleagris* in ancient Greek); it's common English name, snake's head, comes from its bobbing flowerheads. Six narrow, incurved petals form a lovely bell-shaped flower that contrasts with its thin, supple stem. I love its deep-violet colour and checkered appearance.**

At the beginning of spring, you may be lucky enough to see fritillaries growing wild in damp meadows, marshy areas or under deciduous trees, as this is a plant that loves semi-shade. It is becoming ever rarer owing to habitat loss, so you will need to keep your eyes peeled. According to the species, you will see it growing in differing soils and habitats, as well as different altitudes. It is never anything but surprising.

To grow fritillaries in your garden, place each bulb in a hole two to three times as deep as its height. Make sure you place the pointed tip upwards and the roots downwards, and space then 10–15cm (4–6in) apart. Cover them with a little earth.

In spring, you will surely get the chance to admire this precious curiosity of a plant, bowing its head in the spring breeze – perhaps out of modesty.

ILLUSTRATOR:

# Rosie Harbottle

**UNITED KINGDOM**
@ROSIEHARBOTTLE

**If you go on Rosie's Instagram account, you may be astonished to see how often the checkerboard motif turns up in her work. It's as if the fritillary has infused itself into all her work. Rosie likes to say that nature is her muse. Happily for the rest of us, she likes to paint both on canvas and on walls, each time adding her own touch – that little extra something that changes everything.**

Carole: Is it hard to depict the fritillary? Which media did you use for this work?
Rosie: The fritillary is one of my favourite flowers to paint because I love its checkerboard pattern and its 'supernatural' quality. For this work, I used acrylics on a 50 x 70cm (20 x 28in) canvas.

Carole: Why do you think flowers inspire you so much?
Rosie: I've never really thought about the *why*, but I've always had a close relationship with nature. Perhaps it's because my mother's an amazing gardener, or my best friend is a florist. But in any case, I'm attracted by the colours and the organic shapes of the horticultural world. The flowers are so joyous and inspiring that I love to celebrate them in my work.

*If Rosie were a flower, she would be **a dahlia** as she is obsessed by all the different varieties in existence. What's more, she was born in September, the month when dahlias are at their height!*

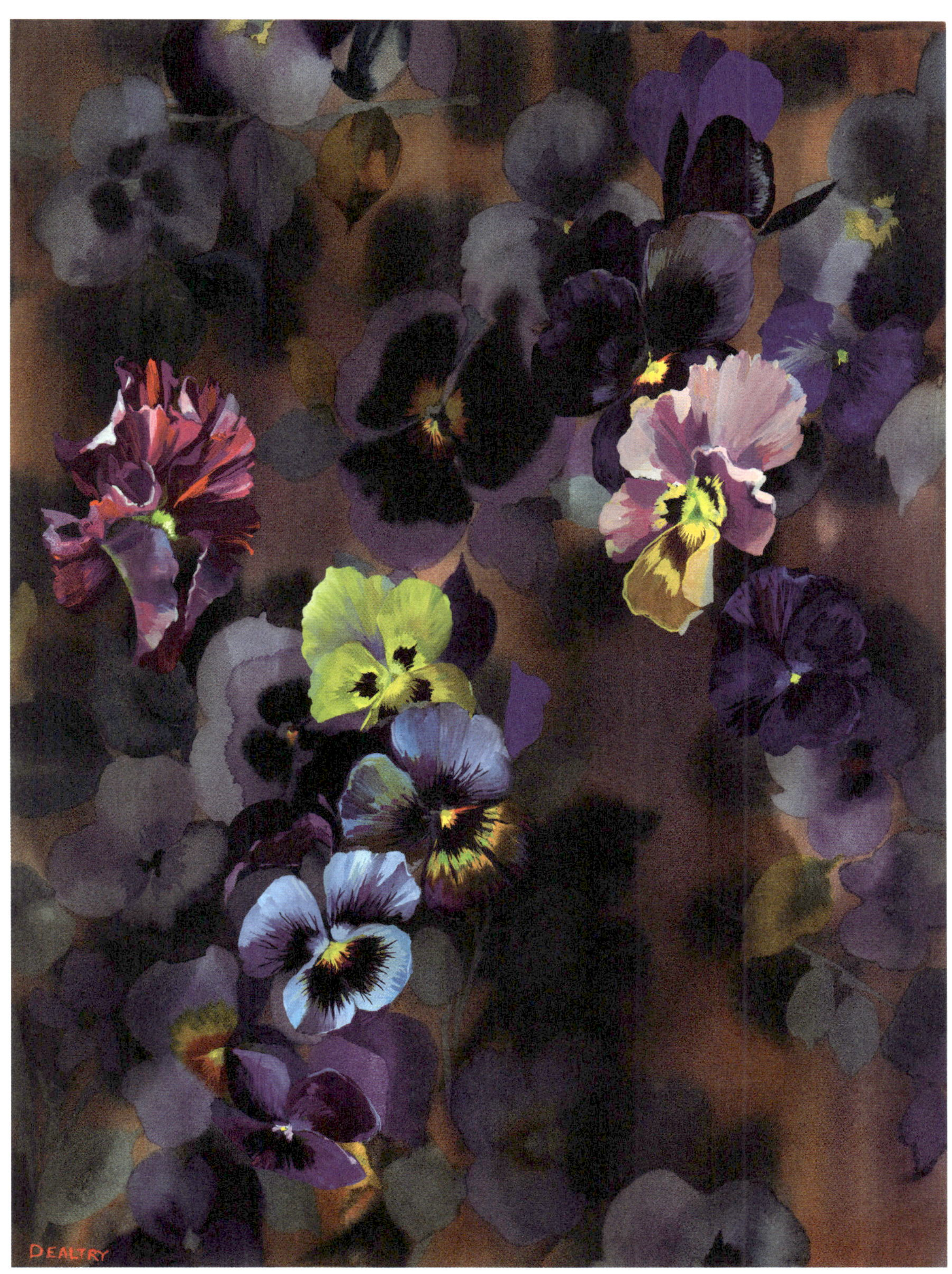
DEALTRY

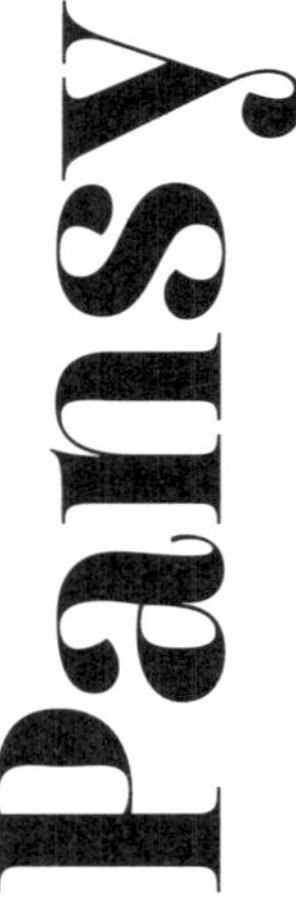


**P**ansies are the colour chart of the garden. With an unbelievable array of colours and colour combinations these small flowers (15–30cm (6–12in) tall) make a big splash – in terms of their contribution to the garden and their popularity. Just saying their name might immediately conjure up the violet-and-yellow variety, but there are numerous other colourways, too. So, if you want some originality, here are three varieties that may overturn your expectations:
• The psychedelic *Viola* 'Angel Tiger Eye Red', vivid yellow with deep-red streaks
• *Viola* 'Molly Sanderson', draped with a deep-black coat
• *Viola* 'Jolly Joker', the perfect name for this variety's vivid orange petals.

Because pansies have such a big impact, you need to think carefully about how you combine them. These annual or biannual garden plants are perfect for borders, pots and planters, in well-drained soil and full sun or semi-shade, bringing you a bit of comfort and joy all year round.

Pansies have five rounded , unevenly sized petals, and five sepals, with blotches of colour (macules) that are often a different shade from the main petal colour – giving them a highly expressive appearance. The hybrid – half-flower, half-human – singing pansies in the 1951 Disney film *Alice in Wonderland* have entered out collective imagination. I confess that their anthropomorphic quality scared me a little when I first saw this film, and even today I'm afraid to eat a pansy flower in a salad!

---

ILLUSTRATOR:

# Helen Dealtry

**UNITED STATES**
@HELENDEALTRY

**Originally from Surrey, England, Helen is today based in New York. She is a multidisciplinary artist and designer and presenter of *Art in Bloom with Helen Dealtry* (on Max, repeated on Prime). She's definitely one to look out for.**

Carole: What media did you use for this illustration?
Helen: Watercolour, ink and gouache in successive layers, using studies of the pansy as my starting point. But I also added a dose of imagination, too. My hope is always to capture the essence of a flower. Here I wanted not only to emphasize the playful aspect of the pansy's macules, but also to give them a velvety, gothic depth.

Carole: Why do flowers inspire you so much?
Helen: I have always been attracted by their dynamic mix of colours. I also take inspiration from their resilience. That the most beautiful specimens can grow in a rock crack or in the driest landscape never fails to offer a lesson to humanity: flowers are bearers of hope.

*If Helen were a flower, she would be **a crocus**, as it is one of the first signs of life after a long winter.*

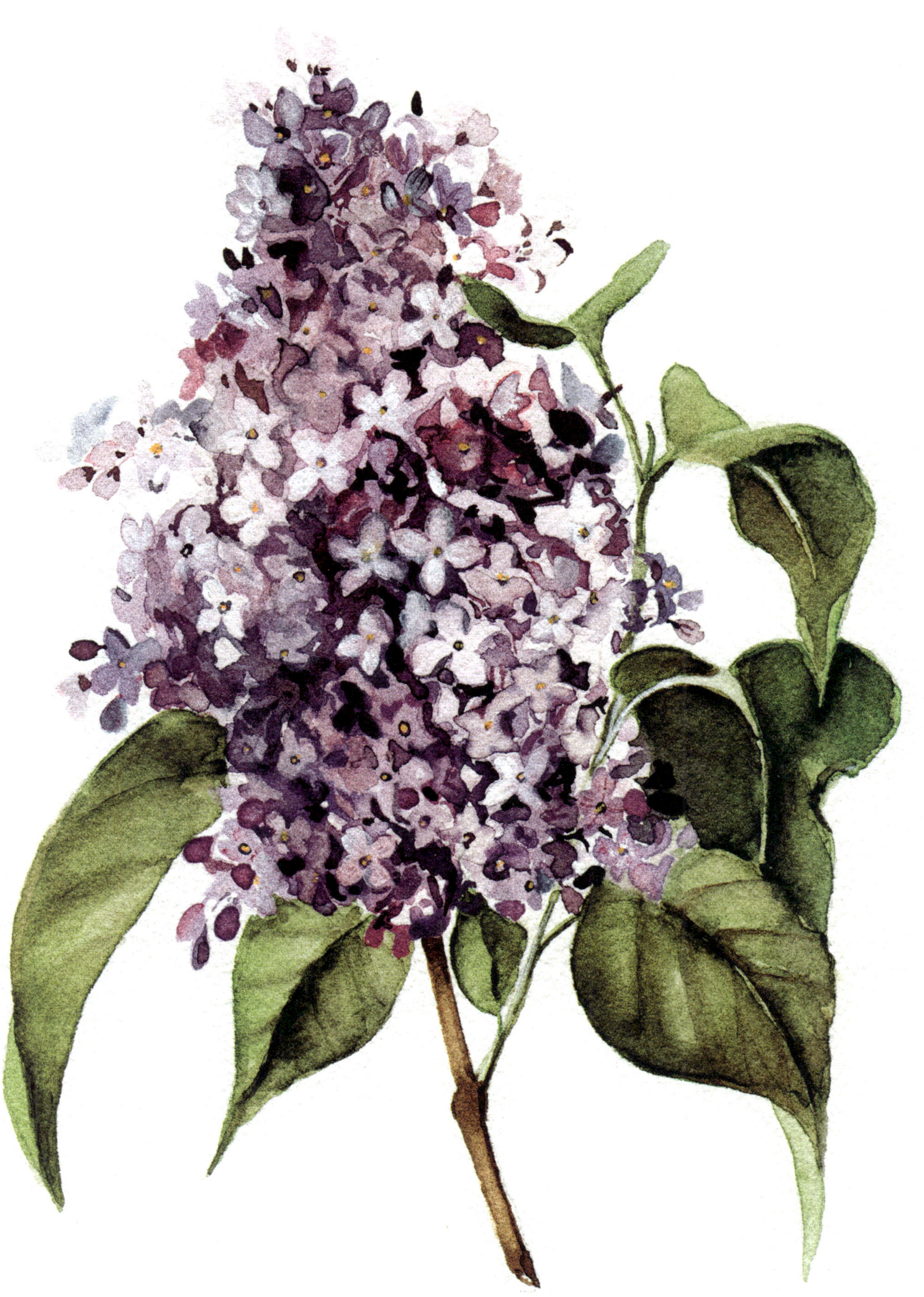
Shealeen Louise

LILAC

**BOTANICAL FAMILY:**
OLEACEAE.

**BLOOMS:**
END OF APRIL–
BEGINNING OF MAY.

**WHEN TO PLANT:**
AUTUMN.

**COLOURS:**
WHITE, MAUVE, BLUE,
PINK.

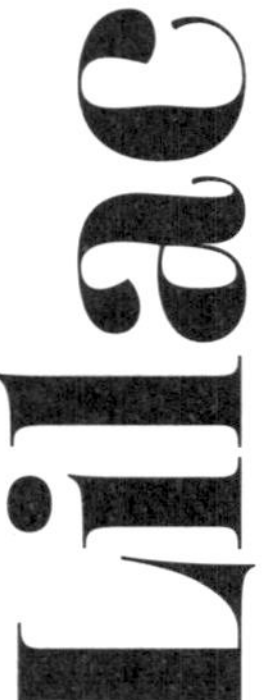

# Lilac

**I**f I were to mention the names 'Madame Lemoine' or 'Madame Florent Stepman', you might think I was talking about your French teachers back at school, but in fact these are varietal names of the lilac, whose scientific name is *Syringa vulgaris*.

I love to see lilac mingling among other shrubs, especially in hedgerows. It has handsome deciduous, heart-shaped leaves, can reach 7m (23ft) tall, and cohabits well with many plants.

The lilac is easy to establish. It's drought-tolerant and blooms profusely, if briefly. *Note:* since the lilac blooms on the wood of the previous year, it should not be pruned in autumn; the buds for the following year's flowers are already present.

When cutting for display, use secateurs to make a vertical slice 3–8cm (1–3 ½in) up the stem and twist one half backwards, or else crush the stem with a hammer. This will enable the cut bloom to take up more water. Remove the leaves along the length of the stem so the plant does not exhaust itself hydrating them.

My favourite lilac variety is 'Katherine Havemeyer', with its pinkish mauve buds and white flowers. I love its old-fashioned charm and its name that sounds as if could have belonged to an English teacher at a French *lycée*.

---

ILLUSTRATOR:

# Shealeen Louise Bishop

**UNITED STATES**
@SHEALEENLOUISE

**Shealeen Louise takes her inspiration from the spring flowers of her garden in New Mexico and the botanic studies of the great French illustrator Pierre-Joseph Redouté to create this magnificent watercolour of a lilac branch on cotton-rag paper.**

Carole: Do you think lilac is a hard flower to depict?
Shealeen Louise: Painting lilac flowers might be hard, so it's important to simplify their form as much as possible. There's no need to paint every little detail.

Carole: Why do flowers inspire you so much ?
Shealeen Louise: They are an explosion of colours, varieties and graceful movements. Everything a painter likes to capture in their work. But I particularly like the way that they reflect back our own strength and fragility. I am especially touched by flowers like lilac that last for such a short while. We should cherish them for the time they are with us.

*If Shealeen Louise were a flower, she would be **a coneflower**. She loves it not only for its many, especially therapeutic, benefits, but also because it grows in the desert. It grows profusely in New Mexico.*

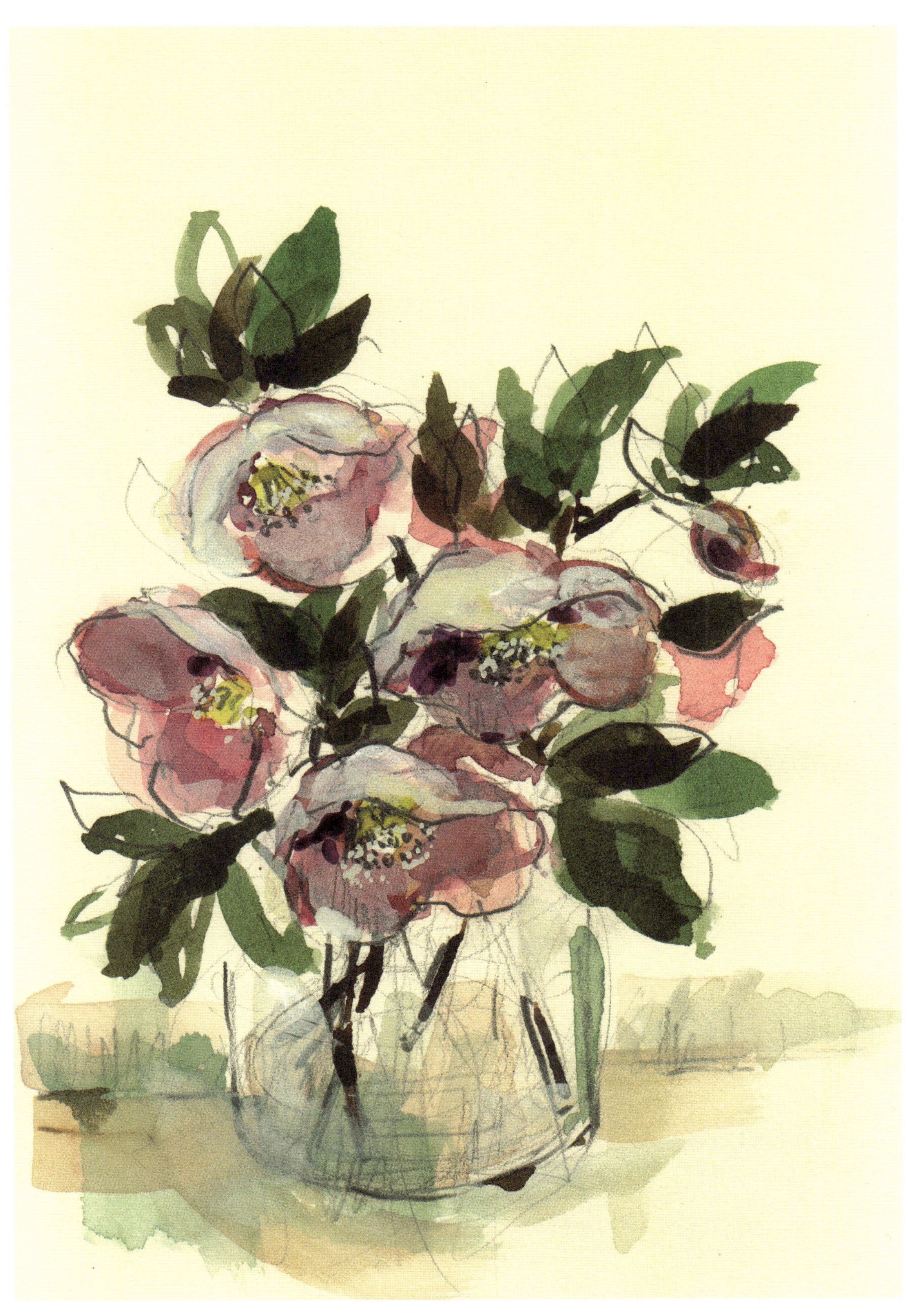

HELLEBORE OR
CHRISTMAS ROSE

---

**BOTANICAL
FAMILY:**
RANUNCULACEAE.

---

**BLOOMS:**
DECEMBER–APRIL.

---

**WHEN TO PLANT:**
JANUARY–MARCH.
SEPTEMBER–
NOVEMBER.

---

**COLOURS:**
WHITE, GREEN, PINK,
PURPLE.

# Hellebore

**F**ritillaries, snowdrops and hellebores – the perfect trio to lift the winter blues.

This charming flower with its big, rounded leaves keeps its flower head bent, making it seem timid. And yet it is so feisty! It can cope with temperatures as low as -15°C (5°F) (according to the variety). Sometimes known as the buttercup's cousin, it is fearless of the cold and blooms continuously for weeks on end, even months.

The hellebore prefers a shady spot, so that it avoids getting its leaves burned. For a hellebore that can flourish in full sun, I recommend the *Helleborus x sternii* 'Flame', a hybrid of the Corsican hellebore (*Helleborus argutifolius*) and the Corsican hellebore (*Helleborus argutifolius*). It is a pretty variety whose colour changes – from violet to pink to green. There are many hybridized hellebores, all rather lovely in their way, so chose the one that suits your soil and position in the garden.

In general, hellebores prefer neutral, or somewhat alkaline, soil, but they can adapt to slightly acid soils, too. Make sure the soil is rich in humus and, most importantly, well-drained. The hellebore's roots should not be allowed to sit in water.

While we are on the subject of roots, it should be noted that the hellebore needs space to develop its root system, so think carefully about where you place it.

---

ILLUSTRATOR:

# Claudia Lowry

**UNITED KINGDOM**
@CLAUDIALOWRY_ART

**Whether her motif is a wildflower of the countryside or a variety from her own garden, Claudia takes her inspiration from nature and can glorify a floral specimen with just a few strokes of her pencil. Here she has given us her interpretation of one of her favourite flowers.**

Carole: Can you explain the behind-the-scenes work that went into this painting?
Claudia: In terms of media, I used pencils, watercolour and gouache. For the motif, I used my own photographs, as hellebores were not in flower at the time. All the same, I should say that I much prefer working from living plants.

Carole: Why do flowers inspire you so much?
Claudia: I love them dearly. Their colours, their shapes, the way they change through the seasons, from bud to wilting flower, are an endless source of inspiration. I grew up in the countryside with parents who loved nature and gardening. It somehow feels imperative for me to capture the beauty that surrounds us.

*If Claudia were a flower, she would be **a snowdrop** or **a primrose**, unpretentious flowers that nonetheless bring a luminous beauty especially at a rather sombre and dismal time of year.*

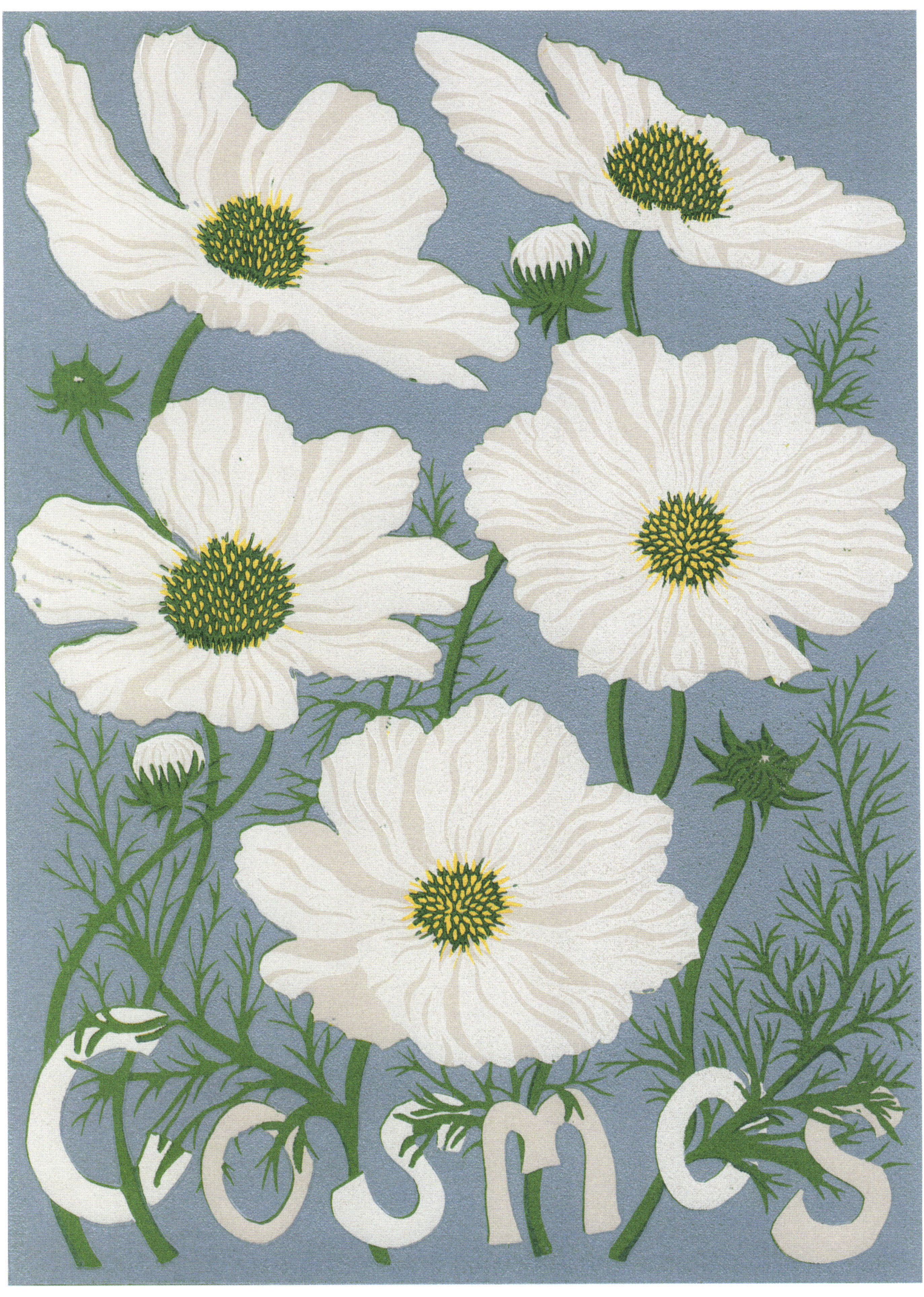

Cosmos

COSMOS

**BOTANICAL FAMILY:**
ASTERACEAE.

**BLOOMS:**
JULY UNTIL THE FIRST AUTUMN FROSTS.

**WHEN TO PLANT:**
SPRING.

**COLOURS:**
WHITE, RED, PINK, PURPLE.


**H**ere is some gentle poetry for your garden and walls. Because of its airy elegance, the cosmos can lift your mood in a moment. Like anything of such pure beauty, it has an unbelievable fragility. At the top of each fine, twisting stem sashays a graceful flower. At the wind's whim, cosmos flowers tirelessly sway.

In the garden, these annual flows will bloom in summer in full sun and then keep going until the beginning of autumn. They need well-drained soil and frequent watering. It is recommended that you mulch to keep the soil cool in summertime.

Other than that, this plant is easy to grow, as long as you can keep away the slugs – as our illustrator well knows: they will gobble up the young shoots as soon as the seeds germinate.

A member of the daisy family, cosmos will bring not only a touch of originality but also joy and harmony to your garden and home.

ILLUSTRATOR:

# Grace Gillespie

**UNITED KINGDOM**
@GRACEGILLESPIEART

**Grace started making lino prints during the COVID-19 pandemic. In lockdown at her parents' home, she spent her time in their garden observing the diversity of flowers and the variety of colours on display. For this work, Grace has embedded the name of the flower in the illustration, something she does not typically do. She began to entangle the letters with the foliage and liked the result more and more. I myself will never get tired of following each stem to its topmost bloom.**

**Carole:** Tell us how you went about this work?
**Grace:** I used the 'reduction' printing method to make this illustration. The outcome looks very much like a normal lino print but you print the various layers of colour from a single linoleum sheet, one on top of the other. It's essential to line up the paper carefully each time, so that your lino meets the paper at exactly the same place. I generally start with the lightest colour and work towards the darkest, until the work is complete. For my *Cosmos* print I used five successive layers, all the while taking full advantage of the colour of the paper.

**Carole:** Are you inspired by the flowers in your own garden?
**Grace:** Yes, though usually my cosmos plants don't grow well because of the slugs and snails. This time, though, I was astonished to find that my cosmos flowers survived the onslaught. I took several photos as references and then began to draw.

*If Grace were a flower, she would be **a hardy geranium**. It may not be especially glamorous, but she is fond of its resilience and ability to endure! What's more, she too loves to hibernate in winter …*